Unlikely Friends

Lessons in Leadership:
The Beginning

By Emi Burke

Dedication

This book is a heartfelt tribute to every soul who has touched my life, whether by imparting profound lessons or by inspiring me to venture down paths less traveled. My journey would not be complete without my parents, who taught me the invaluable lesson of embracing my authentic self, and my husband and children, whose unwavering love and belief in the impossible has filled my life with warmth and joy. Conor and Wendy, two remarkable teachers, illuminating my path from different worlds. One, a little boy whom the world overlooked, and the other, a vibrant presence that captured attention from afar. I am eternally grateful to be their student, for they embody true hope and have shown me the extraordinary power of perseverance and resilience. I carry immense gratitude for the privilege of walking this road, which has unveiled a beautiful truth: we all possess a unique calling, a life assignment waiting to be fulfilled.

—Emi

"*There will always be people who will try to strip you of your dreams and misdirect your journey before you begin. Their negativity is not a reflection of you but a lack of their own focus because they are looking for a reaction. When you face uncertainty, stay the course and carry on. Remember, the sun will always come out.*"

~ *Dr. Murakoshi, Emi's dad*

Introduction

There are moments in time when we must let go of everything we know in order to build the life we are meant to lead. Each of us bears a unique calling, a purpose that beckons us to rise and shine. There will be phases in our lives where we are besieged by self-doubt, questioning our significance, our worthiness. In such moments, we must look inwards and revisit the valleys and peaks of our journey, the instances that kindled our spirits and those that extinguished our hope. To lead a life steeped in authenticity, joy, optimism, and happiness, we must focus on the speck of light in the darkest tunnels and recognize the potential in dreams that others fail to see.

As my Conor would assert, and to which I wholeheartedly concur: no stride is too insignificant when the aim is to keep moving forward, one step at a time. The journey of life unfolds through a series of interconnected events often leading us to our purpose, our life assignment. The real question we must ask ourselves is: what anchors us in the harbor of complacency, preventing us from sailing towards the horizon of our true potential? This is the story and evolution of the Happy Hope Factory, a dream come true built on grit, determination, perseverance – and the unlikeliest of friendships.

With joy & hope,
Emi

Chapter 1

February 21st, 2007, was a most picturesque winter day, complete with cascading, hefty snowflakes reminiscent of the kinds you would find in a holiday snow globe. I got our three sons ready for the day, their spirits as merry as ever; each of us blissfully unaware of the seismic shift in our lives that was looming. Life with the boys was a continuous roller-coaster ride, filled with the simple joys of living in the country and new outdoor experiences each passing day. We had

meticulously laid plans for our future, envisioning the boys playing basketball together, family bike rides, and little Conor running to keep pace with his older brothers as they sprinted up the sprawling, quarter mile-long gravel driveway leading to our house in the clearing. With my husband, Kevin, traveling for work nearly half the time each month, I found myself at the helm of our household, managing everyone's schedules, requirements, and desires. While it could all be quite daunting at times, we did our best working as a team of five. We had all the makings for a very charmed life.

That February day was on course to be filled with joy and excitement, but the long-awaited visit to the pediatric developmental specialist was all it took to steer us into a dark tunnel with seemingly no exit. This day would mark the end of a regular life for Conor, our youngest, and the dawn of a reality that bore no resemblance to the one we had so carefully charted for him: a future brimming with boundless possibilities. There would be no basketball team or chasing his brothers up the driveway.

Conor's life, which we had imagined with limitless opportunities, had been changed forever by the sudden onset of constant seizures. Watching him lie motionless on the floor for months drove me to the brink of madness and compelled me to embark on a quest to find a doctor who could offer solutions and, maybe, a cure. On countless sleepless nights, I scoured the internet for explanations to unravel the mystery surrounding this seemingly flawless child. Standing in the doctor's office, a wave of relief washed over me as I was confident that together we would decipher this enigma. For months, I had constructed a hopeful scenario in my mind involving our hospital visit. I envisioned the doctor stepping into the room, briefly examining our son, and then devising a clear and efficient treatment plan for his recovery. But I was entirely mistaken, and my universe started to crumble around me.

The doctor, sporting a long white coat, entered the sterile, cold examination room and began running a few tests and asking Conor questions to which it was clear he didn't understand or couldn't respond. Without making eye contact, he sat back and began sketching a diagram on a piece of paper, drawing four circles and jotting down the terms SIT, CRAWL, WALK, SPEAK. The doctor's solemn expression, the uneasy shuffle of papers, and the sudden heaviness in the room all started to feel suffocating. As I watched in disbelief, he took his pen and drew a big black X over each term he had previously scribbled within the circles. A sudden knot formed in my throat and tears began to cascade down my cheeks. I was in a state of utter confusion. What the hell was happening?

"In my professional opinion, Emi, Conor will be blind, he will never walk or speak. He will not know that you are his mother," he finally said. His delivery was flat and unemotional, as if he were dictating a grocery list or some other mundane task. But every word of his pierced through me with white-hot intensity. My heart filled with a whirl of emotions – confusion, dread, and profound sorrow. I saw our dreams for Conor instantly slip away, replaced by a new reality that seemed too stark and cruel to bear.

I could see the doctor's lips continue to move but his words were incomprehensible. I needed to escape from here with my baby. I could once again feel tears mounting in my eyes, but I held them back this time, refusing to give him the satisfaction of seeing me wounded by his words. I detested him, despising him with every ounce of my soul. I wanted to yell out, but no sound came.

Holding Conor close, I expressed my gratitude for the doctor's time but emphasized that his prognosis would never define Conor's life. With that, I rushed out, desperate to find a quiet corner to hide in and disappear. By this point, I was in a state of complete breakdown, my hysteria triggering the attention of the security staff who offered to escort me to the parking garage. Reaching the car, I felt a moment of relief within its calm, quiet interior. I snapped Conor's car seat into the base and climbed into the driver's seat, taking a few deep breaths to try to slow my pounding heart.

Epilepsy had entered our once-perfect world, and these invisible adversaries wreaked havoc inside Conor's mind while simultaneously stripping us of our hopes and dreams for our family. Three grueling years lay ahead, where our beautiful baby waged a relentless war against these unseen foes. The harsh prognosis hinted at impending blindness and a lifetime of immobility and silence; the reality of it all was too much to bear. I will never forget, nor forgive, the doctor's blunt assessment that Conor would never improve, and it would be best for all parties if we found institutional care for him and moved on with our lives.

To this day, I still wonder how a doctor could be so casually cruel. I was consumed with an internal fury, longing to tell him how mistaken he was. Was he not aware that my childhood dreams had always revolved around being a mother? Did he not understand that the future I envisioned for my children did not involve seizures, blindness, or a lifetime of dependence?

By the end of 2007, my existence felt like a rudderless ship caught in an unforgiving storm. With two rambunctious toddlers and an infant battling frequent seizures, parenting consumed every bit of attention I had. Kevin's demanding travel schedule meant that the brunt of the caregiving fell on me. Meanwhile, Luke and Cole were largely shielded from the chaos, engrossed in their own worlds of mischief—scenes reminiscent of Dennis the Menace-type adventures generally involving mud, cats, and the playful antics and boundless energy of boys aged three and five.

Looking back, the boys were a great distraction to the emotional turmoil that surrounded Conor. One morning, just after breakfast, I found a note scribbled in the cryptic penmanship of a child attached to a rectangular glass fish tank on the driveway, providing instructions meant for our unsuspecting UPS driver. Jaja, our adventurous male cat, appeared serene within his makeshift enclosure, adorned with a few stray blades of glass and a mesh grate sealed with an overzealous amount of duct tape. I'm sure he was silently thanking me for arriving to liberate him from yet another escapade. The reality was that every moment buzzed with activity whenever those two boys were awake.

Although the boys provided much-needed comic relief, the weight of my anxiety was a constant presence. I was fortunate to have a few close friends nearby who acted as informal mental health supports. In hindsight, they may have needed some therapy themselves after being my sounding board during those emotionally charged tea times. Night after night, as the boys slept and the house quieted, my fears grew louder. I was consumed by the possibility of Conor slipping away into the terrifying unknown if he had another massive seizure, a fear I still live with daily.

Each morning, while steeping my tea, I couldn't help but fixate on a certain spot of my kitchen counter that held a haunting memory where, amid a ferocious snowstorm, paramedics had discovered Conor in a lifeless state. Despite its innocuous appearance, the dated baby blue speckled Formica counter was a brutal reminder of his first severe seizure that irrevocably altered our lives. I grew to despise it, not only for its aesthetics but more so for symbolizing the fragility of Conor's existence. Overwhelmed by the desire for change, I explained to Kevin the urgent need to remodel our space and transform the surroundings that held memories of those difficult times. Alas, even a brand-new kitchen couldn't vanquish the ghosts of the past and, eventually, we sold the house we had once deemed our forever home.

Eager for a new start, we found ourselves relocating to Massachusetts, with Kevin's job acting as our anchor and the exemplary medical facilities in Boston providing a beacon of hope for Conor's care. Our comprehensive relocation deal ensured we had a dedicated realtor to aid our search for a new home in this unfamiliar state. The swift sale of our Maryland home pressured us into a cramped 1,200 square foot rental, half the size of our previous space. This temporary residence, which we jokingly called the "pincher bug house," due to its close quarters with nature's less-than-welcoming inhabitants, heightened our urgency to find our next permanent home. Armed with the determination to secure a new family home within a single weekend—ambitiously over Memorial Day weekend, no less—Kevin and I, along with Luke and Cole, embarked on a trip to Cape Cod. Our mission, however, was dampened by the sudden realization during an hour-long crawl teeming with holiday tourists to cross one of two bridges that provide access, that living on Cape might pose risks during critical situations. With Conor's wellbeing as our top priority, we swiftly shifted our home search to areas off Cape.

My typical resolve kicked in after a futile six-hour home search with the realtor, and later that night once our family was asleep, I sat down to work in the hotel's business center. Combing through hundreds of listings, I was determined to locate our new and final home. The following day's quest was a whirlwind, whisking us from sea-sprayed shores to venerable homes that looked as though they had leapt from medieval storybooks, complete with stoic gargoyles and neighbors shielded behind towering fences. We probed each nook and cranny, ultimately arriving at what would become our residence: a seemingly neglected structure with a scathed lawn and barren interiors where only the first floor was even partially finished. Yet, beneath its unremarkable facade, I saw a potential sanctuary. It stirred a reminiscent joy akin to the adoration I felt for the elaborate dollhouse my mother had handcrafted when I was seven. This was more than a building, it was the future heartbeat of the Happy Hope Factory, with ample room for a burgeoning workshop. The house was ours by the second day in Massachusetts, and within two months we had breathed life into its once barren spaces. It was a massive change of plans, uprooting our three kids to a state far from family and mostly unfamiliar to us, but it was the change we desperately wanted. We trusted ourselves to embrace this new opportunity and make the most out of what would come next in our journey.

Chapter 2

From an early age, I was convinced that my purpose in life was to color the world happy. This ambition was stirred by my mother and grandmother, both wonderful and professional artists with distinct world views. Their influence kindled my curiosity about art, its relation to the world, and induced me to spend hours doodling, drawing and creating

colorful pieces of artwork. I believed my crayon masterpieces, when shared, could spark joy and happiness in others' hearts.

I was also an incredibly shy child, to the extent that I would rather go hungry than order a hamburger at our local McDonald's. The fear of stuttering and being laughed at left me petrified of interacting with the world outside of my home and family. And I was all too aware of how different I was outwardly, too. My mother is white and my father is Japanese, and growing up as a biracial child who looked different than all of my friends was a lonely existence.

There was one day each year that I always looked forward to, a chance to camouflage myself and blend in among my classmates: Halloween. My mother always relished the opportunity to put her creative skills to use and, for this, my kindergarten Halloween costume remains one of my most memorable. Wearing a black plastic trash bag adorned with pipe cleaner whiskers and holding a beachball, I was completely confused at my reflection in the mirror once my mom let me open my eyes. "Emi, you're a circus seal!" she announced with a smile.

I was thrilled at the thought of blending in but also standing out for having the coolest costume in my class. While my more affluent peers wore their fancy store-bought costumes, mine appeared to be the only one that was crafted at home. This distinction didn't escape anyone's attention. Glimpses of walking down the long, musty hallway to my classroom and hearing the whispers from other students still linger in my mind. I could have felt mortified, embarrassed, and alone but I trusted my mom and the love she poured into crafting that distinctive "Trash Bag Seal". I wore it with pride even as some laughed, and I look back at that day as one of my earliest lessons in the power of trust in the face of skepticism.

From an early age, our parents instilled in us the belief that the most valuable contribution we can make to society is kindness. Our father, a renowned pediatrician in the Baltimore area, was widely respected for his gentle demeanor towards his patients. Every weekend, our father would take my sister, Krisi, and I along to visit his pediatric patients at the hospital. Though I was quite young, I could see my father's profound empathy towards these young patients. An absence of cheerful toys and playthings, the kinds I had at my home, was something I noticed as well.

Our mother dedicated her existence to nurturing our artistic and purposeful sides. She exposed us to a range of activities, including tap dancing, painting, and piano lessons - experiences we initially resisted but would later come to appreciate. We led a bustling life that barely allowed for idle moments. However, during quiet nights, I would allow my imagination to wander and dream about my future. By the age of six, I was already aware of the path that lay ahead. I knew then that my life's mission was to bring happiness and hope to those in pain and most in need of encouragement.

The first time I remember voicing my dream out loud was in elementary school. My teacher's face is still vivid in my mind, as well as the sound of her heels clicking on the floor tiles. As she made her way around the room asking each of my classmates about their future aspirations, I readied a unique response. The room buzzed with the energy of my classmates, eager to announce their ambitions: doctor, lawyer, astronaut, teacher, businessman. The respectable professions were many and varied. The wave of responses moved from the back of the room, finally reaching me at the front. I was usually the most reserved, often letting others respond to the teacher's queries. But on that day, I was ready to stand on my own.

When it was finally my turn, I sat up straight in my chair, my heart pounding in my chest. "Emi, what would you like to be

First Happy Hope Bag

one day?" Surveying the room, I observed that my classmates had contributed nothing of the same magnitude. I voiced my dream softly, "I want to color the world happy and brighten the days of sick kids by giving them toys and crayons to make their hearts smile." There it hung in the air: my dream.

The click-clicking of my teacher's heels stopped, and my classmates looked at me with total confusion. The room filled with an awkward silence as my classmates tried to comprehend the unconventional nature of my dream, their faces were a combination of intrigue and bewilderment. Suddenly, the room erupted into laughter and mockery. Feeling as if everyone's gaze was fixed on me like I was an alien, I was completely mortified and fell silent.

As my teacher paced towards me, my anxiety grew with each tap of her shoes against the floor. I felt an uncomfortable lump in my throat and tears stung the corners of my eyes. Finally, she arrived at my desk and calmly explained that while my dream was a lovely ambition, it was most certainly not a profession. I couldn't color to make sick children happy as my job. There was no way I could reach children around the world; it was simply impossible.

My six-year-old heart was broken by everyone's response, and yet, I had a growing intuition that she and the rest of my peers had grossly misunderstood my aspirations. I was absolutely sure that my purpose was to pursue ways to Do Good and instill hope in young hearts.

Those painful years did not stop my love for drawing although I was constantly reminded of my academic shortcomings in elementary and middle school. It felt as if I were a star-shaped figure living in a world designed for circles, squares, and triangles. Despite the daily struggles and criticisms at school, my parents inspired me to pursue my passion relentlessly. I recall my father's comforting words that even after the darkest days, the sun would inevitably rise again. Many years later, a sunshine symbol would become the logo of Happy Hope, a nod towards my father's constant assurance.

There would be many moments in my life when I felt like giving up, when the hurdles seemed insurmountable and the path forward unclear. During my first twelve years in school, I struggled with every subject. No matter how hard I tried, the concepts just wouldn't stick. I felt defeated and often out of place among my peers. After enduring years of relentless challenges, I came to the realization that the solution lay in collaborating with people whose strengths compensated for my weaknesses, and similarly, my strengths for their weaknesses. And on our weekend hospital rounds, I continued to witness pediatric patients in hospitals who were scared, lonely and filled with anxiety. I knew this wasn't rocket science but could crayons and activities really deliver a boost of hope?

Time marched on, yet the memory of those young, resilient faces in the hospital corridors lingered in my mind, a constant reminder of the calling that had nestled itself within me. An unshakeable conviction grew with me each year, a whisper of destiny reassuring me that my path would inevitably lead back to the essence of my life's mission that had taken root in the depths of my being.

Chapter 3

A few years before Conor was born, an enormous grocery store opened to much fanfare in northern Baltimore County. Housing an incredible bakery, a seemingly never-ending cheese display, a butcher, fish monger, the most beautiful produce, and row after row of groceries for every diet, it was quite an experience to shop there. It also happened to be located approximately halfway between our house in the country and the hospital in Baltimore City where Conor was receiving intensive developmental therapy.

As Conor neared his fourth birthday, his struggles with seizures had seen improvements. While the advancements were modest and often imperceptible to onlookers, they marked a positive trajectory in the management of his undiagnosed condition. He was steadying himself on his feet, embracing autonomy with a zeal where even the whispering trees and playful gusts of wind sparked wonderment. His voice remained locked within,

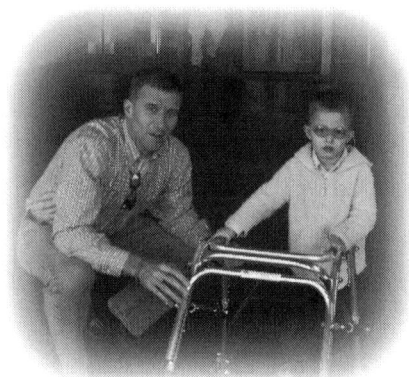

yet his cognitive gears were visibly churning. My heart swelled with joy; we had maybe found some calmer waters after the relentless storm that had rocked us for over four long years.

After countless hours of physical therapy and time spent in and out of hospitals, Conor finally began learning to walk. This was a miraculous achievement considering the bleak prognosis we had received just a few years earlier. And one chilly November morning, after a grueling four-hour physical therapy session, Conor and I stopped at this grocery store again as had become our routine after his therapy sessions. I liked bringing him here because it was so big with nice wide aisles, and it was often slow at this time of day. It was a perfect place to meander on cold mornings with your four-year-old practicing his early steps.

But I had recently developed a second, ulterior motive for scheduling this stop after our regular therapy sessions. Over the last several weeks, I had observed from afar what I understood was a force to be reckoned with. Criss-crossing the store, welcoming patrons while simultaneously directing employees with ease, staging unique shopping experiences for all; as I watched all of this on my visits with Conor, my inner voice started to tell me that Wendy Webster might be "the one". She moved like a fierce lioness, her presence commanding the vast kingdom of her workplace. With the intensity of a watchful guardian, she navigated through her realm ensuring that each of her hundreds of employees felt both valued and motivated. Every glance, every gesture carried the weight of her passion and dedication, inspiring those around her to strive for greatness without ever losing sight of their worth.

Wendy will joke now that I stalked her around the store's tomato display and, well, she's not entirely wrong. I was drawn to what I saw as her incredible knack for leading others, creating unique experiences, and connecting with all. I was certain she was the one destined for me. Every part of my essence declared that all the hardships I had encountered were steps along a path leading me towards her. She was the force I needed to guide me through my next phase of achieving my dream of providing hope to children who were suffering.

Back on that chilly November morning, Conor and I found ourselves walking the aisles of the frozen food section in Wendy's store. As I bent over Conor's diminutive, fragile body, with his tiny fingers clutching the smallest of walkers, I was acutely aware of the struggles he was grappling with, a battle I could never have fathomed even in my most surreal dreams. I had never imagined any of my children having to rely on aids such as walkers, orthopedic braces, or specially designed footwear for the elderly. Despite the heartache over how different Conor's life was from what I had dreamed, I found comfort each night in preparing a miniature suit for him to wear the following day. Perhaps it was my way of picturing a future where he would flourish. He often sported khakis, a pin-striped button-down, a cozy vest, and a quirky bow tie. With miniature gold wire rimmed glasses to correct his strabismus, passersby often cooed over how he was the cutest little professor. Together, we were an unconventional pair in the frozen food aisle: a well-dressed toddler that belied his age standing next to his weary mother in sweatpants, a ponytail, and not a dot of makeup. But it was of no concern to me; my only priority was that pace at which I carefully shuffled Conor's feet, coaching him through each step, teaching him how to walk.

It became evident during our walk that Conor was irresistibly attracted to the gentle hum of the cooling units and their frosty surfaces. As he extended his hand to caress the chilled glass, I stood astounded. For upwards of three years, he had been locked within his own world, incapable of expressing even the most basic desires or requirements. Observing Conor autonomously reaching out to make contact with the icy glass was nothing less than extraordinary. In no time, he began to abandon the support of his walker, tentatively taking one step at a time, leaving behind tiny sweat-dampened handprints on the pristine freezer doors.

While I stood in stunned silence watching Conor slowly make his way along the freezer doors, Wendy appeared at the other end of the aisle. There's a saying that the teacher appears when the student is fully prepared for the lesson that life intends to teach. Looking back, this was the moment that would significantly alter both of our life paths. As Wendy neared, my heart rate nearly tripled and I found myself hastily explaining that this was the first time this small child was trying to walk unassisted.

"That's excellent! I was about to introduce you to John, a valued member of our team who wouldn't mind cleaning the freezer glass doors right behind your little man."

As Wendy stooped to greet Conor, I found myself explaining some more, "Conor doesn't talk. Not yet anyway. He's also mostly blind, so his interactions might not be what you would typically expect from a child meeting someone new. Regardless, he's happy to meet you."

I was deeply moved by the simple kindness in acknowledging my often-invisible child, and that day was a turning point. Wendy had just met Conor, the boy who would inspire her to embark on an unparalleled mission aimed at transforming the lives of countless children. Taking a deep breath, I summoned the courage to ask Wendy if she could spare just five minutes for a chat over coffee. She agreed. Little did I know, that simple meeting would mark the beginning of a transformative friendship, one that would blossom in the most unexpected ways and completely change the trajectory of our lives.

At last, I had found my collaborator, someone who believed in my mission and had the business savvy required to make it a reality. Wendy's presence was a balm to my spirit. Her unyielding optimism and fearlessness in the face of potential setbacks, along with her reassurances that striving for the extraordinary rather than settling for the ordinary was entirely acceptable, bolstered my courage. She was the final element needed to complete my vision. And I can say from experience, there is no better place to encounter your mentor than your local supermarket.

Chapter 4

The vision for what would one day become a Happy Hope Bag began to take shape during the many visits Conor and I made to Wendy and her store. My attention was always split between watching Conor practice taking steps with the aid of his walker and brainstorming the whats and hows of making my vision a reality. Conor's perseverance inspired me every day and I grew fiercely determined to debunk the doubts of my skeptics.

Throughout this journey, Wendy shifted from someone I admired from afar to a guiding mentor in my life. Always the wise one in any gathering, she offered counsel that seemed to echo with the weight of ages, dispensing wisdom even amidst her own chaotic moments. As days morphed into months, the Happy Hope Bag concept began to crystallize. The purpose was straightforward: assemble a modest pack filled with trinkets and toys to brighten the hospital experience for children. It was a simple mission with meaningful implications; these bags would serve as a beacon of hope for children who were suffering and their loved ones. As someone deeply familiar with the experiences of young patients in hospital hallways, I had grown attuned to their silent stories. I could easily read the weariness in their idle waits or the apprehension in their tight grips on parental hands, a testament to their unspoken needs. Through consultations with Child Life specialists, we curated a selection of fundamental items that would form the core of these bags: coloring books, crayons, bubbles, and stampers among others. While the concept was clear and the mission well-defined, we needed a vital element: a name that would perfectly embody and showcase the spirit of our project.

It was on a quiet, early evening walk with Conor snug in his stroller that inspiration struck. Every push of the stroller elicited a joyful cry from Conor that harmonized with the evening choir of birds. Totally defying expectations, Conor, who was once predicted to never speak or communicate, was communicating with me and sharing his wonder and joy at the world around him. His vocalizations took on a meaning deeper than I would have ever expected, standing as a simple yet profound message of hope.

Our charity, the newly anointed Message of Hope Foundation, was on the verge of becoming an official entity. Nonetheless, this entailed maneuvering through the complexities of IRS registration, necessitating the procurement of both financial and legal assistance. I had become an actual information sponge, absorbing all I could from whoever had insights on initiating and funding a charity.

It was my passion project, perhaps bordering on obsession, causing me to spend many late nights parked in front of my computer doing research. I awoke with these children on my mind; they were with me all day and were my last thought before I fell asleep at night. I was consumed by this and shared my vision with anyone who would listen, fueled by an unwavering determination to make it a reality. The entrepreneur's mind is indeed a unique one - a place where fear, uncertainty, and reality are often overridden by ambition, fervor, and grit. In retrospect, I see now that there was never any obstacle that could have stopped me. It was around this time that I stumbled upon a beacon of hope: the University of Massachusetts Law School program offering assistance to locals setting up a 501c3 charity. I seized the opportunity and arranged a meeting with the lead professor. One year from that pivotal day, the Happy Hope Foundation (then called the Message of Hope Foundation) was granted its 501c3 status.

Each night, back at our home base, I would share with Kevin the tiniest indications of progress from Conor, like a self-propelled movement of the leg, or a hand reaching unaided for the freezer door. I would bring to life my conversations with Wendy, wholeheartedly believing that she held the magic ingredient to help me reach my aspiration of serving 200 children in the future. Nonetheless, Kevin, my lifelong partner who had lovingly supported me in every possible  way and had always been the voice of reason, would tactfully remind me of Wendy's own responsibilities and the unrealistic expectation of her abandoning her own dreams to follow mine, regardless of her potential contribution. Still, I had a strong sense from somewhere deep within that there was too much momentum now for this vision to not become reality.

———

During a routine check in with my obstetrician-gynecologist back in Maryland—the one who had delivered Cole and Conor into the world, and who had worked tirelessly to comprehend Conor's developmental challenges—I brought along Conor. My physician was more than a healthcare provider; he had become an integral person in our lives akin to family, and someone who shared in our heartache. In the exam room, Conor moved around with a clumsy determination, his knee-high orthotics concealed in diminutive orthopedic shoes. His delighted squeals echoed in the room, marking a stark contrast to the solemn visits of years past where he lay motionless in a wheelchair. When the doctor stepped in and caught sight of Conor bursting with life and curiosity, his attention was immediately captured.

His expression registered sheer astonishment as he exclaimed, "Emi, what a surprise! And who might this young man be?" Before I could muster an answer, tears began cascading down my face. "This is our Conor," I managed to say, my voice trembling with emotion. "Don't you recognize him?" His voice softened, almost to a whisper, "Emi, this is nothing short of miraculous. To think that he's standing here, free from his wheelchair; it's beyond what I had dared to hope for." My doctor stepped outside, promising to return in just a moment.

The minutes stretched on, each one feeling longer than the last.

Finally, he returned, his eyes moving from me to Conor and back again. With a mix of bewilderment and excitement, he shared how extraordinary he thought Conor's progress to be, and he invited me to consider speaking at an upcoming medical symposium where Conor's story might be of significant interest.

The mere idea of public speaking was daunting; I had spent the last 1,278 days singularly devoted to my son's well-being, clad in my uniform of sweatpants and simple ponytail. The concept of indulging in a solitary shower on any kind of regular basis was completely foreign by now. And the idea of squeezing myself into something considered "business casual" felt like a most unwelcome chore. Nevertheless, I knew that the strides Conor and I had made together could be a beacon of encouragement to others. With a slight hesitation, I accepted the invitation for a one-off presentation.

However, as news of Conor's breakthrough spread, my life drastically changed. My schedule was soon packed with flights crisscrossing the nation, from Boston to San Diego. I, who had once shunned even the smallest amount of public attention, was now recounting our story before packed rooms of medical professionals—including some of our harshest skeptics. With each session, I shared our unwavering hope and the belief that each of us has a gift which can transform the world.

After a speaking engagement one evening, I was gathering my possessions and making my way towards the car when a doctor and his wife approached. He explained how my story had moved them, and that they shared in my vision for what the foundation could be. Then he handed me a neatly folded check. Until that moment, the idea of fundraising was an unfamiliar territory to me; I had been funding everything from my own pocket. I expressed my deep thanks, grateful for what I assumed would be a small token of support. But as I sat in my car and looked at the amount, I was floored. The check was for $250, accompanied by a napkin note that boldly declared: NOTHING IS IMPOSSIBLE. MAKE IT HAPPEN.

Overwhelmed with joy, I knew I had to call Wendy. This was a miracle, and I wanted her reaction in real time. From the parking lot of Ruth's Chris steakhouse, I eagerly dialed her number to share the good news. Wendy's response was instant and ambitious, "Emi, that's amazing! Now, set your sights higher. For 100 kids, you'll need $2,500." Her words hit me with the force of a sledgehammer. I was barely wrapping my head around $250, and now she was pushing me towards a goal ten times that amount. Reflecting on that conversation now, it's clear that Wendy was just priming me for even greater possibilities ahead. Very soon, the opportunity to spread the message of hope propelled me onto a bigger stage: a national conference in San Antonio, the most significant platform I had yet to encounter, and this time I would be on my own.

Stepping off the stage post-presentation, my gaze fell upon the CEO of the hosting organization making his way towards me through the rapt audience. With purpose in his stride, he ascended the platform and extended a firm hand in congratulations. There I stood beside this colossal figure, scanning the crowd as hearts swelled with anticipation. "My aim," I mustered, "is to create joy for 200 hospitalized children with happy bags full of toys." Applause rippled through the room as I unveiled my lifetime goal. Yet, in a sudden shift, the man beside me was poised to raise the stakes. I had never envisioned surpassing 200 children; simply assembling 10 bags alone by lamplight, my nightly routine of indulging in reality TV while packing my dollar-store treasures, felt monumental.

"Emi, your vision inspires us, and to show our support, we've procured 20,000 'Hope Happens' yellow drawstring bags, set to arrive at your doorstep next Friday." I stood there completely stunned, envisioning Kevin opening our front door in shock as an array of colorful bags tumbled endlessly over our doorstep. And indeed, that following Friday, that vision became my reality; before me stood an ocean of yellow sacks, a gift that had, quite literally, appeared on my doorstep.

The whirlwind of unexpected generosity I was finding myself in was exciting, and a little overwhelming. Before I had even put out a call for donations, people were contributing funds and products in droves. It was all hands on deck, and naturally, I reached out to Wendy for her keen insight. "Wendy, I'm swamped with 20,000 yellow knapsacks. My basement is going to burst at the seams, and I don't have nearly enough supplies," I explained in a frenzy. "Relax, Emi," she replied calmly, "we need to put this to the test. You've got connections in Baltimore. Let's put together an event and call it the Baltimore Hope Factory." And so, we did.

Upon my arrival in Baltimore the next week, Wendy and I hit the ground running, pouring every ounce of energy into engaging the Baltimore community for what promised to be a remarkable occasion. The plan was to accumulate specific supplies at a local church who had donated space, and I planned three informational sessions to stir up community involvement and energize everyone to bring along their networks. It would all culminate in a Baltimore Hope Factory event where we'd pack 200 bags in a single day.

As awareness of the upcoming event grew, I anticipated a surge in donations — crayons, stickers, and coloring books amassing at the church doors. Surpassing my own past records, I had successfully raised $7,000, but a new thought crossed my mind: what if the generosity of our community resulted in contributions exceeding 2,000 toys? Rather prematurely, perhaps, I took it upon myself to contact the local supply chain carrier for potential assistance with our assembly line and distribution of the gift bags. After several unreturned calls to the plant manager, I decided to make an in-person visit.

Once inside the logistics hub, I navigated to the office, ready to present my proposal. As I approached the front desk, I greeted the receptionist and asked to speak with the plant manager. However, I did not have an appointment. The receptionist was kind but firm, informing me that without an appointment she couldn't grant a meeting, but she would relay a message for me.

Despite my escalating frustration, I made one last attempt and explained, "Listen, there's a charity event coming up in a few weeks, and I'm on the hook for a pretty big task. We're set to assemble 200 care packages for children in Baltimore who could really use a reason to smile. I need your team on board - not just to help with packing, but also for handing these out to the children. I'm ready to camp out right here until I can speak with the manager, because trust me, I'm not going anywhere until we have a chat."

So, there I was, camping out in the lobby with each minute stretching out endlessly. After what felt like an eternity, out stepped Joy Howard, who was a spitting image of Wendy. With friendly confidence and a radiant smile, she got to talking. "Alright, shoot. Why are you here and what do you need from me?" Surely, I thought, after an hour of committed rehearsal, my pitch would glide out smoothly. Yet, in Joy's presence, my rehearsed words vanished, my gut instead indicating a much more crucial revelation: "EMI, here stands your ally #2". And thus, history unfolded. Joy, alongside Wendy, became my dream team. Two powerhouses united towards a common goal, frequently reminding me, "We're here for backup, Emi, but you're the one in the trenches." I understood what they meant, loud and clear. And so, with determination, I stood ready to captain our collective endeavor.

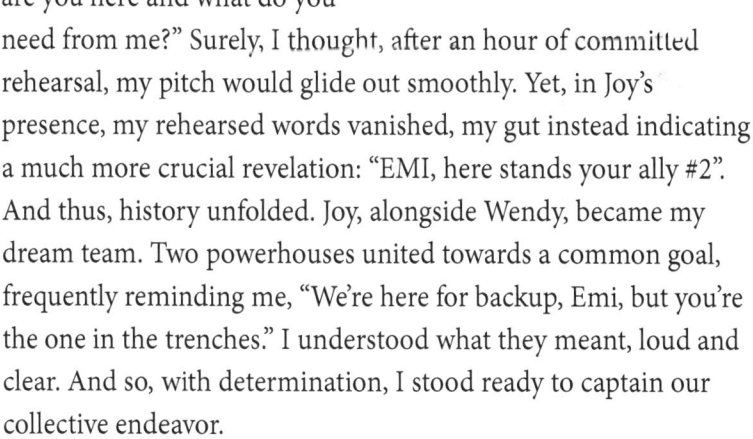

Back in Massachusetts, I rallied my social media networks to chip in funds or donate supplies in advance of the big day. With a digital army of volunteers shepherding the counting and organizing of contributions, my excitement paralleled the days of crabbing on the Chesapeake Bay as a youngster. The energy was similar: my father, shaped by a childhood in Japan during tougher times, had honed his love for freshwater fishing on the side of a stream. Now, in command of our humble boat, we'd dedicate our weekends to mastering the catch. The thrill lay in the unknown – both beneath the waves back then, and now, beyond the church doors where the collected treasures awaited.

After enduring an eight-hour drive with my minivan groaning under the weight of countless crayons and drawstring bags, I arrived back in Baltimore in advance of the event day. My van, now with damaged shocks from surpassing its weight capacity, was nothing compared to the shock I experienced as I approached the church. A member greeted me with an offer to help just as I was about to enter. Confidently, I mentioned my connection to the Factory event and inquired about the donations. To my surprise, she mentioned that the toys had been temporarily stored outside in a van. This was in stark contrast to my vision of toys spilling out of every door and window.

My mind was racing as we walked towards the parking lot. I had envisioned a mountain of shopping bags spilling over with children's toys. Surely, the van was just for excess items, with the building already brimming? Peering into the utility van, my confusion mounted; just a few bags lay within. I turned to the woman, our puzzled expressions mirroring each other's.

"I'm a bit lost here — I can only see a handful of bags in the van. Surely, the rest must be inside, right?" she suggested with a tone of hope. Yet when we ventured back indoors, only a sparse collection of small Target bags greeted us, each with but a few items nestled at the bottom. My heart sank.

Fearful of facing the community empty-handed—and the bleak prospect of no hope bags for the children—I hastily retreated, seeking refuge in my 'mom mobile,' cumbersome and Griswold-esque as it was. Fumbling for my phone, I dialed Wendy's number and started rapidly filling her in on what just happened.

"Emi, I'm confident that the community will come through with donations. Just hang in there," Wendy tried to reassure me. "Look, it's already 8 pm. You're worried, which I get, and we've got $7,000 at our disposal for supplies. But let's not rush out just yet," she advised. Wendy's suggestion to grab pizza instead was met with little enthusiasm from me. Even though food is my love language and pizza is always a treat, my appetite was nonexistent.

Anxiety gnawed at me all night long and I couldn't shake the visions I was having of this first event failing in such a disappointing way. Perhaps the concept wasn't robust enough, or maybe it called for a savvy entrepreneur rather than a determined mother. Struggling with an onslaught of fear and doubt, I found myself walking back to the church on what was supposed to be the preparation day before the main event. Arriving an hour before the others to get ready for the first group of five volunteers, I opened the door to the simple room,

furnished with just a handful of tables and chairs. The church staff greeted me with open arms, their encouragement a balm to my frayed nerves. "Emi, tomorrow is going to be wonderful," they reassured me. "This is exactly what our community needs." I managed a smile, secretly wishing I shared their optimism.

Despite my initial hesitation, Wendy's voice echoed in my ears, "They will come." And they did. Our gathering soon mirrored a scene akin to a modern-day loaves and fishes tale, with community members appearing en masse, arms laden with toys for those less fortunate. This event unfolded as a testament to the pure-hearted generosity of people and cemented my faith in humanity – and in our mission. The day was punctuated by moments of sheer grace, none more poignant than witnessing a young man crafting a heartfelt card for a hospitalized child, the paintbrush gripped purposefully between his teeth. Confined to a wheelchair but undeterred, I watched as he carefully held a bag while his caregiver assisted him in filling it amidst the bustling crowd of volunteers at the packing lines. My eyes welled up with tears as I saw his determination to contribute despite his own personal challenges. It reminded me of my Conor, whose life also mattered despite his outward appearance.

And yet, amidst this joyful scene, I felt a tap on my shoulder and a woman introduced herself, requesting a private conversation. Anticipating a personal anecdote or even a possible contribution, I followed her out into the hall. She started off with praising the concept of our event but criticized its execution. In her view, including individuals with disabilities was hindering the overall progress. She proposed we halt the process, send all non-essential volunteers home, and continue only with the most efficient packers. I suppressed the impulse to seize her shoulders, wanting to jolt her into realization. "This isn't about self-importance or productivity," I would say, "it's about every individual contributing to change through their actions." I knew there was one very special person that this woman needed to meet to help make my point.

As soon as the lady paused to recharge her lungs, I motioned for Wendy to come over and join us. I last glimpsed the woman being guided out the door, and she never joined us at another event. But she did serve as a reminder of an important life lesson. No matter how many rainbows you're trying to paint in the world, there will always be people trying to rain on your parade, criticize your masterpiece, or begrudge you and your bravery. But know that their criticism does not define you or your vision; it's imperative to keep your head high and understand that your ideas, skills, and dreams can transform lives because YOU believe in them.

The communal spirit that day was palpable as hundreds gathered, united by a shared goal of spreading goodness and hope. Amidst many heartfelt stories and laughter, the legacy of our beloved Conor became clear with his influence reaching out to touch the lives of other struggling souls. On that significant day, supported by an outpouring of goodwill, we not only met our goal - but we also soared past it, packing 2,000 bags of hope. In the depths of my being, I knew this path was true.

Chapter 5

The success of the first Baltimore Factory event supercharged my ambition and excitement, and with the help of my community at home a Massachusetts Factory was held soon after where another 2,000 Happy Hope Bags were packed for hospitalized children. After that, it was full steam ahead. Donations began to pour in, with some (crayons, stickers) more useful to children than others (pantyhose, press-on nails).

My daily routine quickly formed around postal runs and packing my momma minivan with boxes to sort at home into our now-familiar ten categories. Despite the challenges in raising funds for new purchases, every parcel seemed to carry with it small acts of kindness – folded dollar bills, small handfuls of change, and thousands of pennies. It all played a part in our mission, taking us one step closer to delivering happiness to hospitalized children. My frequent visits to Target's $1 Spot soon became a cornerstone of our inventory efforts, amassing a treasure trove of items in preparation for our much-anticipated annual events.

Thankfully, I struck up a friendship with the manager of Target who often saw me clogging up the checkout lanes with my numerous purchases of crayons and coloring books. Curious customers would sometimes mistake me for a teacher, while now and then, I'd catch a glance of annoyance from someone who mistook me for the grinch as I lugged multiple carts to the registers. Things came to a head when I managed to fill five carts with over a thousand items, leading our local store

to kindly arrange after-hours shopping so they could open two registers just for my enormous haul. Companies began contributing stuffed animals to the cause and, committed to never turning a donation down, I spent days shuttling from one generous donor to another with my van packed so full the boys could barely peek out from between the bags of gifts. This continued for several years, putting a strain on both my back and the trusty minivan, until we realized it was time to improve our operation and begin producing our own line of products.

Our campaign to spread cheer through handwritten cards had reached an extensive audience, with students from every corner of the country eager to contribute to our cause of delivering happiness. We created a card writing campaign that started off with heartfelt and uplifting messages filling every card. These cards would flood to Hope Central, my residence, but quickly my mailbox could no longer keep up which prompted a kind suggestion from our local postman to opt for a post office box. We were overjoyed to receive heaps of cards weekly. However, tucked amidst the well-wishes were a few inappropriate outliers. Just as our earlier list of approved items for donation received unexpected additions, the cards, too, began reflecting a deviation from our guidelines. One striking example was a card that proclaimed on its cover, "I'll be proud of you for anything you do in life", which to our dismay was followed by the inappropriate caveat inside, "unless you become a stripper." This incident made it clear that it was time to pivot our strategy, leading to the decision to supply our own pre-printed cards, which would only leave space for the individual to color the card and sign their first name.

The level of generosity from strangers overwhelmed my heart, especially from children around the world who simply wanted to be a part of making a difference. As a fierce storm brewed outside one winter, I posted a photo of a Rainbow Loom bracelet sent in by an eight-year-old who wanted to share a little kindness. Little did I know what a stir that one photo would cause, and soon our quaint Cape Cod post office was inundated with rainbow loom bracelets from every US state and cities around the world. Initially at a loss for how to properly clean these gifts, we resorted to laboriously washing them one at a time, eventually progressing to massive batches in sizable containers, drying them in the expanse of our entry hall. The bracelets, and the countless tiny loom pieces, seemed to take over our home and we spent two years distributing over a quarter-million pieces of woven joy. We were in awe of how this one simple gift seemed to inspire so many to reach out and learn more about our mission.

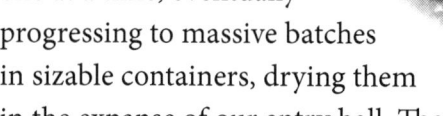

Children from every corner of the country were sending handwritten requests, calling with inquiries about getting involved, and emailing with ideas for projects. School campaigns collecting essentials and Dress Down days for fundraising took off with great success, laying a solid foundation for our endeavors. However, as our ambitions grew, so did our strategies. Corporations began calling and it became clear that there was a unique opportunity to collaborate with corporate entities. By offering team-building experiences as a mutually beneficial exchange for their philanthropic support, we could expand our impact and provide value on multiple levels. To expand our reach and truly grow, it became clear that we had to start producing our own materials.

The inception of our branded Hope Hero card marked a pivotal moment for our foundation; it symbolized not just our own creative design but also promoted a culture of kindness, where the young recipients are encouraged to extend gratitude towards their supporters, be it medical staff or family. This very card remains a staple within our Happy Hope Bags to this day. The arrival of the first batch was a milestone: our own artwork and insignia embellished on those cards that reached our doorstep, signaling the tangible reality of our Happy Hope branded product. This momentous occasion left an indelible mark on me, and it wasn't long before we introduced the 'You are Special' card. This card, infused with color by volunteer hands, conveys a heartfelt message to the children: that they are cherished members of their community.

––––––

Back at Hope Central, our staff consisted of a skeleton crew that was just me, volunteering full-time without pay. To handle the volume of inbound calls, I had set up a toll-free number that streamlined calls to a handful of extensions: for donations, press 1; inquiries, press 2; item collection, press 3; and so on. Each prompt ultimately rerouted back to me. While my mentors, Wendy and Joy, were available for guidance, they were deeply entrenched in their professional careers, managing large-scale operations. One unassuming day, I got a buzz on the hotline from a woman, "Hello, is this the Hope Factory?" This was a first; our modest promotional efforts had only been a small stash of homemade leaflets, produced by my own black-and-white desktop printer. I responded with a cautious, "Yes, it is. How may I assist you today?"

The reception was staticky, and I grew immediately suspicious when she proposed a partnership with a $15,000 event budget. This was an obvious too-good-to-be-true hoax. Convinced this was Wendy pulling my leg with an elaborate prank, I hung up. Without missing a beat, I immediately phoned Wendy, ready to catch her mid-prank with a playful accusation. But I did not at all expect her reply that she had been in a meeting and hadn't called me. My joking tone dissolved into mortification as I processed her words, and she urged me to return the call. I did, realizing that opportunity had indeed been knocking on my door – and it was legitimate. This episode turned into our inaugural, and now longstanding, corporate partnership with Blue Cross Blue Shield. Do I wish I hadn't hung up on my first potential major sponsor? Well, yes. But once I overcame my embarrassment, I was able to reset our budding relationship with a mixture of gratitude, humility, and excitement.

In the forthcoming months, my journey involved visiting companies that were open to hosting our events, with a twist in the regular model. They gathered the materials, I kickstarted each gathering, followed by a communal pack-a-thon. The end product: bags full of hope, which I would personally deliver to a number of local hospitals while dressed in my Hope Fairy tutu.

Typically, these events were hosted pro bono, and on occasion I'd notice Wendy's watchful gaze dissecting the event and making observations to discuss on our drive home. Running on fumes from these altruistic yet unsustainable efforts, a strategic pivot was necessary. "Emi, it's time to face reality," she would eventually tell me. "The Hope Factory is a hit, but we're bleeding resources. We need a sponsorship model in order to keep serving children." I balked at the idea of charging companies to host Hope Factory events, but I also knew she was right; I had to muster the courage to make it work.

With regular events in Maryland and Massachusetts, the operation often saw us shuttling products in our trusty minivan and fashioning makeshift assembly lines wherever we could find space, from cafeterias to office lobbies. Requests for our Happy Hope Bags started pouring in from hospitals across all 50 states, each call echoing a pressing need: children without the most basic of necessities like a toothbrush, or those in long-term care left to the monotony of television for lack of recreational activities. The call for hope was undeniable, but the challenge was daunting: how could we secure funding and establish connections in communities we weren't physically present, especially given that we had no staff to dedicate time to these activities?

Determined to scale our impact, it was time for some creative thinking. I researched numerous courses and mentorship programs before settling on applying to a well-regarded accelerator based in Boston. I could not have imagined then the humbling, exhausting, life-changing journey I was about to begin.

Chapter 6

After completing lengthy applications, participating in interviews, and endlessly describing my goals and vision for the Hope Factory, I finally made it to the final stage of the accelerator's application process and was invited to present my cause. This stage generated no fear in me; I had honed my pitch relentlessly over the past two years, sharing the dream with anyone willing to listen.

But as every parent knows, when a critical workday arises, it is almost a given that something will happen with the kids. On the date set for the pitch, as fate would dictate, school was out for our 12-year-old son Cole on this crucial day, so he became my impromptu plus-one. My boy had been one of my earliest supporters, keeping me company into the early hours of the morning as he helped with everything from sorting products to unloading supplies. He knew the ins-and-outs of the Factory concept as well as I did. Having him by my side on that day wasn't a worry; in fact, it was a point of pride. I wanted him to witness firsthand that determination can turn dreams into reality.

We arrived full of anticipation, ready to present my brainchild among thousands of contenders all vying for a handful of coveted spots. While waiting in the towering building, Cole glanced at me with a mix of pride and concern, remarking, "Mom, you should know how proud I am. But wow, look at everyone else—so young and polished. I think you're about the same age as their moms."

"First, I want to express my gratitude for your confidence, Cole," I said softly. "Just remember, the individuals we are meeting with are not so different from you or me. They've managed to grasp their ambitions, not unlike your mother has. It's simply that fortune favored them with an early revelation of their path." As my name echoed through the foyer, Cole trailed me, his barely-contained excitement causing the air to buzz with anticipation. Our attendant ushered us into an exquisite glass elevator, soaring to the 17th story, where a panoramic vista of the cityscape enveloped us; it was a breathtaking sight. We proceeded along the corridor, finding ourselves by a pair of chairs just outside the pitch room. A glance through the door's narrow window revealed a young entrepreneur in the midst of his pitch; my pulse quickened, and my stomach fluttered tumultuously, bordering on nausea. With no room for nerves and so much at stake, I gathered my composure, crossed the threshold into the room the moment my name was called, and stepped into the future.

Gaining admission into the program catapulted me into an intense daily routine of envisioning grander possibilities, pushing my limits, and relentlessly searching for ways to bring HOPE into hospital rooms everywhere. My mentors consistently pressed upon me the urgency to expand our reach; their words often echo in my thoughts even in the stillness of night, "Emi, you must find a way to scale your efforts and impact. It's imperative to tap corporate America to support your ideas." During those four months, Carolyn Dias—my trusted confidant and the Foundation's appointed CFO—and I would journey into Boston. We faced a 20-minute trek to the train station followed by an hour-long train ride, all the while singularly focused on a persistent conundrum: how to scale up our impact.

Finally, I had the breakthrough idea we needed. Imagine if we could encapsulate the essence of the Happy Hope experience into a deliverable box, enabling teams from any location within the United States to contribute and participate. The innovative Happy Hope Box concept allowed teams to gather within their workspaces, such as break rooms or around the conference table, to assemble the Happy Hope Bags at their convenience. This brilliant solution solved the issue for those who wanted to contribute but were tied to their offices and couldn't participate in external activities.

I remember the sense of excitement and pride flooding in as I dialed Wendy to share the news. She, practical as ever, prompted me: "Set a tangible goal, Emi. How many companies will receive these boxes monthly, and how many bags will each assemble? Strategy is key." It took some experimentation, but we figured that including 25 bags in each kit for a $500 donation was the optimal arrangement, equating to $20 per bag. Initially, I was skeptical about the feasibility of selling even one box, but Wendy's insistence on a 'pay to play' model for sustainability was convincing. Keeping her counsel in mind, I dared to aim for four boxes a month which equated to $2,000 in monthly revenue. The next challenge, though daunting, was a necessity: convincing companies to contribute financially to a project they used to support voluntarily. But Wendy's advice was clear; scaling up the initiative required investment.

Day by day, as the boys were immersed in their schoolwork, my hours were consumed by pouring over various corporate social responsibility initiatives and mustering the courage for my most dreaded activity—cold calling. Yet, with each call, my understanding of how companies structured their charitable efforts and defined their foundational philanthropic values deepened. The very notion of dialing a complete stranger's number sent my stomach on a queasy rollercoaster ride. But, giving up was not an option. Admitting defeat seemed far more intimidating than the calls themselves, considering the time and hope Wendy had infused into my project. This was a challenge I would have to tackle head-on.

———

The four months spent as part of the accelerator were nothing short of exhilarating, a dream come true as I navigated the train rides to Boston each day. Each journey felt like a pilgrimage as I sat amidst a brilliant group of young visionaries, their minds ablaze with transformative ideas that could redefine our future. The mission I set for myself was to connect with as many mentors as possible, pouring over the list of entrepreneurs and arranging meetings whenever possible. Each one I scheduled felt like another critical step towards moving the foundation into its next big phase. I was determined not to let a single opportunity slip through my fingers, driven by the knowledge that every interaction could hold the key to something extraordinary.

I had the incredible privilege of meeting individuals from all walks of life—legal experts, finance wizards, and creative minds from the entertainment industry, each with their own unique stories to share. As I immersed myself in a whirlwind of 80+ meetings over the course of my time there, I found myself driven by a relentless desire to find a way to expand our operation. The thought of bringing others into our mission to pack Happy Hope Bags consumed me; it was a constant companion in my thoughts. The more I reflected on it, the more I felt an undeniable spark of hope. The excitement was palpable, and I could almost taste the success that lay just beyond the horizon.

Even though we ran the current operation from the dimly lit basement after my children were tucked into bed, I could vividly envision a thriving Happy Hope Factory blossoming within my dreams. I pictured everything so clearly—the bold Factory signage proudly adorning the exterior, an inviting entryway that welcomed all, and the joyous swarm of volunteers, their smiles radiating a shared purpose and commitment. Logistical trucks brimming with brightly colored Happy Hope boxes delivering hope to those who needed it most. And there, amidst it all, were the children, their eyes lighting up as they received our thoughtfully crafted therapeutic activity bags. This vision ignited a passion within me, a heartfelt obsession inspired by the profound belief that hope could truly change lives.

One of the last steps before completing the program at the accelerator was to meet with a final mentor to discuss the next stage of your project, one that would be pitched to a room full of program mentors later who would then decide who was a finalist, and whose project was a winner. Heart racing with a mix of excitement and anxiety, I arrived for my meeting an hour early, my mind a flurry of thoughts as I aimed to find clarity and focus.

My experience in the program had been exceptional. It was incredibly challenging mentally and emotionally, but I knew going into this that I had one opportunity to give it my all— a promise I made to myself which I faithfully kept. As she approached, I stood up with anticipation, reaching out for a warm handshake, hoping to share a moment of genuine connection. Instead, she slid into her seat without a word; her demeanor was as cold as ice and it left me reeling, acutely aware of the invisible barrier she had erected between us. My heart raced as I scrambled to find the right words, desperate to unearth even the faintest smile hidden beneath her steely exterior.

"Emi, I read your bio and your vision for the Happy Hope Factory. I see that you dream of a brick-and-mortar space filled with supplies and volunteers eager to help assemble bags," she started. "Frankly, it's the worst idea I've ever heard here. It's not viable and, really, a waste of everyone's time." Her words were like a stab in the gut, slicing through my dreams and leaving a wound I hadn't anticipated.

My mind was racing, haunted by the chorus of "no" that had echoed throughout my life—the voices of those who tried to dim my light, leaving me questioning my worth and drowning in self-doubt. I could vividly recall my third-grade teacher, her harsh words piercing through my childhood hopes: she didn't believe I would ever graduate high school, let alone set foot in college. Then there were the cruel classmates from that lavish all-girls Catholic prep school, their laughter ringing in my ears as they vandalized my space, tossing my plaid uniform and loafers into the toilet as if my very existence was a joke, calling me 'Buddha Baby' because of my mixed raced ethnicity. In that moment, I felt the weight of their scorn pressing down on me, a heavy reminder of all the times I had been belittled and overlooked.

This time around, I was firmly planted in adulthood, grappling with the immense challenge of building a business that had the potential to transform the lives of children in hospitals and shelters. This wasn't just a fleeting school project; it was a mission I was deeply passionate about, one that I genuinely believed could make a meaningful difference in the world. As the woman unleashed her harsh criticisms, cloaking her venomous words in a guise of expertise, I felt a surge of anger rising within me, a near-volcanic eruption that threatened to spill over. Despite the turmoil churning inside, I chose to remain composed, listening to her relentless diatribe until I could bear it no longer. With a steady breath, I politely interjected, determined to assert that, regardless of her skepticism, the Happy Hope Factory was not just a dream but an unstoppable reality in the making.

I gathered my belongings, my hands trembling as I clutched the papers tightly as if they could somehow anchor me to reality. I stood up slowly, each movement feeling heavy, and thanked her for her time, though I felt anything but thankful for her comments. A sense of devastation washed over me that left my heart racing in a cacophony of confusion and sorrow. Tears threatened to spill over as I hurried away, yet amid this tumultuous despair, a flicker of resolve ignited within me. Even if I stood alone, one solitary believer in a dream that others couldn't see, I knew I would never abandon my mission—the very essence of my being, my life calling.

Emi's Hope Hero – Carolyn

Chapter 7

While I did not win over everybody at the accelerator program, I did come away with what I was growing to realize was a winning idea. With a signature box that could be shipped to any location, filled with all supplies needed to pack bags and pre-paid shipping to the local hospital, all available for an accessible donation amount—it would be easy for anyone to do good, give back, and share hope.

As a naturally creative individual, I swiftly concocted a modest, yet meaningful activity box intended for donation to hospitals. Disregarding packaging initially to keep costs down, I sourced Conor's empty bulk diaper boxes from BJ's to deliver supplies to Happy Hope corporate events. The image of sleek corporate settings juxtaposed with the arrival of oversized Pampers boxes still makes me wince in retrospect. The incongruity of professionals toting baby diaper boxes to their desks is a humorous testament to the lengths we stretched in the name of charity during our early years.

Honestly, it never occurred to me to question some of those practices. Every cent was devoted to serving children, and that was what mattered. And companies were ordering; the concept was working! However, even the best of intentions sometimes needs a diaper box-sized reality check. That moment arrived one dusky evening when Wendy was back in town and I was racing the clock, trying to beat the 5 pm UPS deadline at our local Staples for outbound shipments. In a flurry, I swerved the minivan up to the entrance; Wendy leaped out as I flung open the trunk, expecting her to grab the parcels. As she stared incredulously at the sea of boxes, I couldn't help but burst into laughter. "Emi, where are the boxes?" Wendy was truly confused. "You're looking right at them; they're the large boxes in the back!" I exclaimed. "DIAPER BOXES," she retorted, voice escalating, "really, Emi? This is absurd—you cannot expect us to send off HOPE in diaper boxes!" Thankfully, I eventually caved on this one. It went through a few iterations, but our branded Happy Hope Box today is a beautiful package that I'm proud to send out to partners worldwide.

———

Within a short span of two months, demand surged, and we were shipping out six boxes monthly, propelled by the power of word-of-mouth recommendations. By day, my time was consumed with company research, while evenings transformed our unheated basement into a family-run production line where we assembled and packaged the contents for the hope bags. It was crucial that every bag included a personal touch—a handcrafted item that would bring a unique sense of joy to the receiving child, just as homemade gifts had always warmed my own heart. Reflecting on those early days, I admit our maiden projects were simple, featuring things like sticker and cotton ball embellished headbands and rudimentary alligator bookmarks made from tongue depressors with green pipe cleaners for limbs that inevitably tinted our fingers a lime hue—but they were crafted with immense pride and care. We added painstakingly cut tiny teeth, a task that left our fingers sore but notably contributed to the uniqueness of the craft. Despite the challenges, it was an unforgettable endeavor—one I would be hesitant to undertake again. As the movement gained momentum, organizations began to contribute their time and resources to assemble our kits. Each kit included a clear plastic Ziplock bag, a set of Crayola crayons, a small tub of Play-Doh, our handcrafted items, and an assortment of trinkets from Target's One Spot section.

Now that we had perfected the craft of creating our exclusive collection of Hope Hero greeting cards, I was convinced our next essential product should be a custom coloring book. After extensive research, I stumbled upon a company renowned for crafting stunning coloring books for various groups. Initially, the cost for each book was $2.00, but after some negotiation, they agreed to lower the price to $1.50. However, the company informed me that it would cost an additional $2,000 for their artist to design the cover and the pages within. Despite their persuasive argument for using their graphic designer, I couldn't justify the expense, knowing those funds could supply 1,300 children with coloring books instead. Determined to allocate our resources more effectively, I bought a copy of "Illustrator for Dummies" and learned to design a delightful coloring book on my own. In the many years since we first began assembling Happy Hope Bags, we have learned to wear many hats. This stems partly from my inclination to be frugal—not out of miserliness, but from a desire to use our hard-earned donations in ways that make a bigger impact—and partly because we prefer to serve more children rather than spend excessively on services we're capable of learning ourselves. I compiled our first coloring book swiftly and placed an order for 2,000 copies, taking a significant gamble that felt right as a vital step in establishing our brand identity. But then, two weeks later as we awaited the delivery, I got an unexpected phone call.

"Emi, is there a loading dock at your location?" they inquired. "What about a pallet jack?" I was perplexed. I had no clue what a pallet jack was—a device for shifting pallets apparently. As it turned out, every single pallet of coloring books that arrived, and the many that followed over the years, had to be manually offloaded. This led to frustrated delivery drivers, some of whom refused to make the delivery at all. After books were taken off the pallet, they then had to be carted down the driveway using Conor's wagon, box by box. These were indeed trials by fire, taxing in ways that stretched beyond the mental to the keenly physical.

Conor's plastic Fisher-Price wagon was my trusty chariot to haul countless deliveries until the day Kevin gifted me my inaugural dolly. Our home's driveway, a rugged trail of potholes patched haphazardly with crush and run, posed a formidable challenge. Imagine maneuvering a handcart brimming with coloring books, the wobbly tower rising above the height of my forehead. After conquering the outdoor obstacle course, an indoor odyssey awaited—a trek through the kitchen, across family footpaths, and a descent into the basement, our fledgling command post. Those formative times, marked by long hours and the biting chill of basement labor, remain etched in my memory as the period when the bedrock of our enterprise was laid bare.

As our operations burgeoned with corporate engagements and curated box orders, the obvious reality set in: my ambitions outstripped the bandwidth of a solo operative. So, I decided to enlist my neighbor to assist. The financials of sustaining even a modest five-hour weekly assistant left me uneasy, but necessity demanded a leap of faith. Together, with an arsenal of ideas and a ceaseless volley of attempts, we aimed to build the quintessential Hope Box. Despite just as many discarded plans and failed ideas, I held an unwavering belief: continued perseverance would manifest a product not just remarkable, but scalable.

As word continued to spread, we began offering a series of onsite events with our corporate allies, drawing in groups of 10-20 dedicated volunteers for 3-hour sessions at various venues. These events focused on creating our signature headbands using donated stickers, assembling Hope Hero cards paired with Crayola crayons we had bought wholesale, and working on small, thoughtful crafts designed to spread cheer to children. With the upcoming holiday season, I had to quickly adapt when our volunteers showed an eagerness to dive into painting for our charity events. Hiring professional instructors was out of the question since they charged $300 per class—not a small sum for a nonprofit trying to maximize its donations. I was determined to acquire the necessary skills myself, staying up until 2 a.m. to figure it out. I was a bundle of nerves, aware that 45 eager 'Hope Heroes' were anticipating I could guide them through crafting a wintry masterpiece featuring a snowman with a bird. Thankfully, a Bob Ross-style tutorial on YouTube provided me with the crash course I needed. The result? A surprisingly successful painting class and $4,500 raised, with every single dollar going directly to assist children in need.

In the ensuing months, improvisation became our strategy as we aimed to keep both our new and stalwart volunteers engaged. Initially aiming for four boxes a month, our ambitions swiftly expanded as we distributed eight, then thirteen, and soon twenty boxes monthly. The growing demand made it clear: a dedicated space was imperative to sustain and nurture our expansion over the coming years. Our operations had begun humbly with makeshift workstations in the basement, but establishing a more permanent and organized workspace was going to be crucial.

Eliminating the expense of rent, we transformed a substantial section of the basement into a compact yet highly functional Hope Factory within three weeks. Through extensive online searches, I procured several furniture donations, including a sizeable conference table, which became central to our preparation area. A volunteer's grandfather, who brought his expertise as a professional builder, crafted an ingeniously designed packing station. This station, positioned at the heart of the space and featuring built-in drawers, provided easy access to all necessary supplies within arm's reach. Additionally, we dedicated a cozy nook of the basement to serve as our communication hub, handling all order processing from this makeshift call center.

Adjacent to the house stood an exterior staircase leading into the yard, which became the main thoroughfare for transporting materials from the delivery trucks to our mini-factory. Recognizing the need to streamline the process as shipments

increased, we encased the stairwell, which spanned 15 feet in length and 5 feet in width. This enclosure proved timely; every day at 5pm, our reliable UPS driver, Dave, would arrive to collect the outbound

Happy Hope Boxes, destined for corporations eager to make a positive impact in their local communities. Every box that was out for delivery had been hand painted with fresh yellow polka dots, a splash of color that would occasionally transfer to the carrier's brown uniform. Mid-February saw the completion of our basement work area. Despite the absence of heating—and the biting cold that came with it—we were filled with elation over our newly established workspace. The sound of our persistent calls echoed against the chilled walls as we tirelessly reached out to potential leads, and as a result, the demand for our service surged exponentially. Our home would transform

into a bustling hub of altruism, accommodating throngs of eager high school students and corporate do-gooders. With pop-up tables set up as makeshift workstations starting in the driveway and front yard through to the dining room, and  a street lined with vehicles, it was the unmistakable sign of another day dedicated to volunteering.

———

Within just a few months our production had doubled, reaching the milestone of preparing 40 Happy Hope Boxes each month. I pledged to myself to expand the team upon hitting 60 monthly boxes. Surpassing my expectations, we sold 85 the following month. I promptly recruited two part-timers for assembly and design tasks, along with another employee dedicated to corporate outreach. Our efforts quickly bore fruit, catapulting us to a staggering 100 Happy Hope Box events a month—a figure beyond my most optimistic projections when our stretch goal was a modest four. The increased volume turned my UPS driver's pickups into a rigorous evening workout, and the overflowing stairwell of packages was a clear signal: it was time to scout for a dedicated production facility.

To get there, we needed one additional resourceful individual to help amplify our outreach and potentially double our business volume within the next half year. Hiring decisions were challenging—they needed to align with our culture and enhance the dynamic among a closely-bonded, all-female team working in tight quarters. Our aim was to find not just a team member but a beacon of positivity, someone to infuse our days with joy and facilitate our mission to reach more children. I tasked my team to be on the lookout for that exuberant spirit during their daily interactions. To our delight, one of my staff members burst into our workspace the following day, unable to contain her excitement, "I've found the one; our beacon of joy!" It became immediately apparent upon meeting this young woman, an effervescent coffee shop barista with bright red hair and infectious warmth, that she was more than a joy filler—she was a deliverer of hope. The young woman accepted our offer and joined our team the following week, bringing her radiant positivity into the fold.

Our team's synergy had finally hit its stride, and with a personal mantra in mind—reach 150 and we advance—I witnessed our operations humming with efficient precision in the depths of our basement headquarters. Each member exuded confidence within their designated roles, an integral piece of our collective success. Observing their seamless collaboration transported me to childhood memories of marveling at a colony of ants, a united force in diligent labor. Naturally, as any tight-knit group facing the pressures of an expanding enterprise, we were not strangers to conflict or missteps. Yet, through it all, our resilience shone as we not only met but surpassed our goals with a remarkable tally of 175 box orders for the following month.

The momentum was with us and as we diligently worked to bring joy to hospitalized children with Happy Hope Bags, we encountered a new call to action. The hardships faced by children enduring the aftermath of natural catastrophes—hurricanes, floods, and wildfires—couldn't be ignored. Debating the distinction between aiding those in hospitals versus children who might have lost everything was never at issue. Our corporate allies, already vested in our mission, reached out proactively, echoing the desire to assist. It became clear that our response would require adapting our efforts to deliver relief to those affected by such catastrophes. The modified packs would need to include essential items such as toothbrushes, socks, and hand sanitizer alongside the toys and games to carry our message of hope.

Upon realizing the need for a more portable version of our cherished coloring book, I immediately contacted our publishing partner to commission a compact edition that would fit within our yellow drawstring bags. These bags would be essential for the children who had lost much in the wake of disaster and needed something with which to carry their essentials. Despite the urgency, the printing company rose to the challenge, and we expedited shipping to ensure prompt delivery. The arrival of the coloring books was nothing short of a logistical ballet—5,000 copies delivered promptly within two days. While the weighty pallet required unpacking box by box, my husband and sons managed the heftier tasks. Clutching a single box with anticipation, I hurried to the basement, eager to look through our newest creation.

Discovering that all 5,000 coloring books resembled hastily made copies, printed on thin, subpar paper with faded ink was disheartening. Tearing through box after box, I felt a weight heavy in my chest. Distributing these low-quality books to children who had already endured so much felt wrong; they didn't reflect the high standards our foundation had prided itself on. Despite the urgency to include them in the care packages, I instead reached out to the supplier to express our disappointment and the inconsistency with our values.

As I languished on hold, shuttled between various customer service reps, my patience was wearing thin. But then the owner picked up. I poured out my heart to him, explaining how these kids, possibly in the toughest phase of their lives, deserved a high-quality coloring book with crisp lines. I was immediately taken aback by his dismissive response, "If they've already lost so much, they should be appreciative of any coloring book. And if you think you can produce a better one, why don't you just do it yourself?" Those words, meant to be the end of the conversation, instead ignited something in me. "Make one myself?" I echoed. "Yeah, go ahead," he challenged. Within moments, my mind began to race with ideas, and by the end of the call, I was resolved to make it happen.

Two days later, Canon and Xerox had sent their representatives to my basement with proposals for an industrial-grade printing press, the kind that prints 120 copies per minute and staples together office documents. The cost was daunting — $2,500 a month for the lease, plus ink expenses. Yet, the print costs had already been spiraling to more than $5,000 monthly. The numbers made sense; it was logically sound but financially intimidating. As our demands increased steadily, the prospect of moving out of that basement and expanding became an unavoidable reality I had to face.

The cascade of gratitude filled every evening with purpose as Happy Hope Boxes continued their nightly journey up the back stairs, around the garage, and onto the UPS truck. With each box sent out, letters, emails, and phone calls brimmed with accounts of personal victories, emotional odysseys, and heart-touching tales—voices that resonated deeply and left a profound imprint on my memory. One particular call has stuck with me after all of these years. At the end of a long day immersed in packing, followed by an enjoyable family dinner and the bedtime routine for our boys, I found myself back in the workshop to finish the day's tasks. Amidst clearing the packing counters, the unique ring of our 800 number interrupted the silence. "Happy Hope Factory, Emi speaking."

"Emi, your box of Happy Hope Bags arrived last week, and I just had to share an extraordinary story with you." It was a nurse, calling to share with me the story of a young girl's ER visit and how the impact of our work was felt that day. In that moment, every sleepless night, every fret over finances and the relentless sway of doubts that come with any business venture crystallized into a single truth—every step on this journey was making a difference.

The little girl's family in the ER was about to learn of her likely leukemia diagnosis. At this life-changing turning point, the nurse spoke of a moment just before her family grappled with the weight of the diagnosis: a Child Life specialist presented a Happy Hope Bag to the girl. With a mix of curiosity and familiarity, she surveyed the bag, examining the playful contents before revealing a homemade card. "Mom, it's my bag," she declared. Her mother affirmed, "Yes, darling, it is your bag." But the girl insisted, "No, Mom, it really is MY bag." Understanding dawned as the child continued, "Mom, I made this card at the Baltimore Happy Hope Factory. This bag, I filled it with the toys I picked out." Such instances illuminate the profound cycle of giving—an act of kindness that spirals back to us, sometimes in the form of heartfelt compassion or unbridled joy, and once in a rare while, as a direct echo of our own actions, just like the return of one's very own Happy Hope Bag.

———

As our operations scaled up, with packages flying off the shelves as quickly as we could prepare them, our inventory management turned into a real-life game of Tetris. Products journeyed from the storage area, zigzagging through the yard before descending into our basement—a hive of perpetual activity. One evening at half past ten, a tractor trailer with

a delivery of 8,000 Playdoh tubs arrived tragically behind schedule. In anticipation, I negotiated with the boys—a bribe involving a modest extension of their bedtime in exchange for their help in unloading the truck. The delivery driver, upon discovering the joy his cargo would bring to thousands of hospitalized children, was overcome with emotion and the evening morphed into an impromptu celebration with basketball and cheesecake under the outdoor flood lights.

In contrast, we also faced the pressure of high volumes overwhelming our logistics partners. One driver, whose truck was packed to the brim with boxes of pinwheels that were going to necessitate a return trip to his facility for the rest of his regular packages, became severely overcome with frustration. We watched in shock as he began to forcefully drop-kick the boxes off the back of the truck. That moment underscored the stress that even our peripheral team members were feeling due to the soaring demand for Happy Hope Bags.

Handling deliveries only scratched the surface of our challenges. Our factory space was bursting at the seams, unable to contain the influx of thousands of toys intended for eager customers. This led us back to a familiar dance of shuttling goods around the house, seeking any nook that could double as storage, while also trying to keep inventory neatly sorted. What was once Kevin's sanctuary for exercise became the new home to a quarter-million crayons and thousands of Play-Doh tubs, a cacophony of colors and scents that permeated the small space. As each day passed, I grew more certain of our increasing necessity for a warehouse, if the trend of multiplying orders persisted. The strain was visible; our team, composed not of seasoned executives but neighbors and soccer moms, worked shoulder to shoulder. With every unanticipated order, the palpable tension among us grew, as did the anxiety over how we would manage if we continued to grow at this rapid pace. I was beyond proud of the immense efforts that had gotten us to this point, and all-too-aware of how we were at the precipice of the next stage of growth—and how quickly it could devolve into disarray if I didn't start thinking even bigger.

Chapter 8

Most evenings, when the kids were tucked in and the previously bustling house had fallen quiet, I would descend the stairs to the basement and spend some time alone to think and reflect.

This once-empty space where I had initially envisioned processing four Happy Hope Boxes month, a number which had seemed enormous and a milestone of success, was now overflowing. Countless sleepless nights were spent pondering over how to find four corporations to sponsor Happy Hope Bags. Yet, defying at least all my expectations, we found ourselves packing 175 boxes each month from there—a place I had anticipated calling our operational home for three years. But the explosive growth made it clear that our surroundings were far too constrained to keep pace with the surge in operations; change was imperative. And amidst this growing sea of operational need, there was one individual I turned to for solace and direction, my Conor.

Despite his silence, Conor held a profound way of touching the deepest parts of my spirit, a connection so intense it transcends the need for speech. His mere presence brought clarity and direction, like a guiding beacon amidst life's tumultuous waves. He was my unwavering lighthouse through the unforgiving storms, and I often sought refuge from the world to simply be with my child. It had become clear to me that although Conor still lacked the ability to speak with words, he reveled in the sensation of the breeze against his cheeks when I'd take him out in the stroller. Despite my uncertainty about what he could discern visually at such a tender age, his expression would brighten the moment he was nestled inside what would eventually become the jogger. With increased speed came heightened exhilaration; Conor's gleeful squeals as we picked up the pace were a melody that filled my heart with pure joy.

By 2017, Conor had outgrown the jogger, prompting me to explore alternative modes of transport that would accommodate his growing needs. An extra-large bike trailer designed specially to cater to the needs of children like him was a perfect find. Our journeys with the trailer, fastened securely to my bicycle, along the familiar twists and turns of the Cape Cod Canal path, were fueled by his unbridled excitement, signaling our newfound passion with many more adventures to come.

One Saturday morning - July 15, 2017, to be precise - I embarked on a cycling journey that would forever alter the trajectory of my life. The day was notably warm as I stowed the trailer, our bicycles, a modest picnic, and an abundance of water bottles into the car. Upon reaching our destination—

the trail—preparations were meticulous: setting up the bikes, securing Conor appropriately, ensuring his comfort with the fan, and adjusting the mirrors so I could continuously observe his reactions.

The sight of his trailer never failed to impress, reminiscent of an oversized egg perched on a pair of wheels. Fully loaded, the trailer with Conor tipped the scales at about 175 pounds--quite the load to haul, especially over a 14-mile stretch, half of which was going against the wind. We had embarked on this journey five times in the past, so I had no reason to think that this sixth trip would be any different. The path was alive with fellow bikers and pedestrians, all under the watchful eye of graceful birds slicing through the sky and the steadfast tugboats carving through the canal. Setting a brisk pace, we reached the sea in less than an hour and began setting up our picnic. As we dined, I casually mentioned to Cole a weird tingling sensation in my left arm and a gentle numbness within my fingertips.

Always helpful, Cole offered to swap bicycles and take on the task of towing Conor, but I was reluctant to do so knowing the additional exertion needed to haul that much weight for seven miles against the wind. As we set off again, the familiar tingling sensation crept up my arm. Attempting to cycle single-handedly proved challenging, as the headwind fiercely challenged my control over the bike's direction. Dropping my head for aerodynamics seemed like a good idea, but ultimately was futile. The open design of Conor's buggy was catching the wind like a giant parachute, slowing us down to what felt like a crawl. The strain was like hauling an anchor, yet Cole's encouragements rang in my ears—"C'mon Mom, you've got this!"—fueling my determination. I gritted my teeth and pushed on, pedaling with all the might I could summon against the invisible force of a dozen heavy kites. Conor must have sensed that something was amiss, because his characteristic squeals abruptly ceased. The trek back to the car took us an excruciating ninety minutes, leaving me completely drained. I hastily stowed the bikes and buckled the boys into the car, making a beeline for home. I was feeling a palpable sense of urgency in the air, as if we were racing against time itself.

At around one in the morning, I was abruptly awakened by a sharp and searing pain in my back, a sensation akin to flames that quickly surged down my left arm to my fingertips. The intensity was so overpowering that I found myself sitting upright and drenched in sweat as the fiery pain shot through my chest. My arm and fingers began to go numb, triggering an overwhelming sense of panic. I was convinced I was experiencing a heart attack and, attempting to cope with the severe discomfort and fear, I took what seemed to be the most sensible action under the circumstances.

Not wanting to wake anyone in the house with worry, I drove myself alone to the nearest emergency room. Luck appeared to be on my side; the ER was unusually quiet that night, and I found myself in the care of medical staff shortly upon my arrival. Lying on the gurney, I did my best to answer a litany of questions from the doctor while receiving doses of potent painkillers easing my discomfort. They subdued the sharp pains racking my back and chest just enough for relief to creep in. In the haze of waiting for a diagnosis, my mind wandered back to my bike ride with Conor. The memory of his laughter as we raced against the breeze was a vivid contrast to the sterile hospital room. I quietly hoped that this would not be our final adventure together, yearning for many more moments of shared freedom and joy. What activities could we enjoy together, considering one was a boy whose endurance for walking was limited, and who probably couldn't ever operate a typical bike? Letting him down was non-negotiable; I was determined to figure something out. Perhaps the incident wasn't a significant one, perhaps there was no cause for alarm. As I drifted in and out of consciousness, Conor's image remained the steadfast focus of my thoughts.

Upon the doctor's return, his relaxed demeanor had a soothing effect on me. His diagnosis pointed to muscular spasms, and unexpectedly, he advised a visit to a chiropractor. This was a divergence from what I had witnessed growing up with a father in the medical profession, where such a referral was not commonplace. After being released at the break of dawn, I managed to drive myself to the sanctuary of my home and sought refuge under the comforting sheets of my bed. But the peace did not last.

Just a few hours later, I was jolted awake again by a fierce blaze of pain tearing from my back into my chest. Numbness had once again taken over my left arm, igniting a fresh wave of panic within me. I began to realize the gravity of my situation, yet I was caught in a whirlwind of fear, uncertain of what to do next. Tears blurred my vision as I walked the second-floor hallway, wrestling with indecision. With the pain in my chest mounting, the question loomed: should I rush back to the nearest emergency room or make the trek into Boston for care? I've always prided myself on being decisive and proactive, yet in this moment of distress, paralysis took hold, leaving me feeling vulnerable and disoriented. And yet, in that moment of pain, my fairy godmother appeared. Carolyn, the Foundation's volunteer and CFO arrived at my doorstep intending to surprise me with a treat but was met instead with the sight of me distraught and pacing the hallway in tears.

"Emi, what's going on?" she asked, alarmed. "I'm not sure, but my arm is numb and there's this excruciating pain in my back and chest, like I'm being stabbed." Without hesitation, she rushed to her car, rearranged her hefty 90-pound bulldog to make space, and swiftly drove me to the ER of a renown Boston hospital. It was 11 am. For the following five hours, I found myself on a gurney in the corridor, awaiting attention from the medical staff. Despite the overwhelming agony, more intense than the throes of childbirth, I remained acutely aware of the suffering sustained by fellow patients lingering nearby. As my condition worsened, my grasp on sanity began to unravel; in sheer desperation, I sought solace on the cold floor of the examination room. Indeed, in that moment of distress, the grimy hospital floor seemed like a sanctuary compared to the relentless pain.

My concerns had escalated far beyond the discomfort in my back, chest, and arms. There was a growing fear inside me that paralysis was imminent as the sensations began to fade.

I couldn't help but wonder if the many years spent lifting and carrying Conor, before he found his own footsteps, had taken an insurmountable toll on my spine. Perhaps the strain of lugging too many crayon-filled boxes from the driveway, across the lawn, and down to the basement was catching up to me. Or maybe the effort of battling the wind while pulling Conor over the final 7 miles had proven to be more than I could manage. My mind was a sea of worries, foremost among them the haunting possibility that I might fail in my duty to protect my young son entrusted to my care.

Lying on the emergency room floor, I felt increasingly detached, my family waiting at home, my friend in the lobby, and me— unaccompanied in despair. This memory haunts me even now, a stark reminder of why our mission at the Happy Hope Factory to provide a beacon of hope in times of deepest need is so vital. From the floor with numbness creeping throughout my body, I looked beyond the half-drawn curtain to the corridor. There, the eyes of an old man met mine, causing me to avert my gaze momentarily. Curiosity drew my eyes back to him, and as our gazes locked once more, a sense of serenity began to wash over me, calming the storm within. The cascade of tears halted, and the turmoil churning within me all day started to calm. The searing ache that I had been battling eased and I was so struck by the solace of the experience of human connection. Silence enveloped us, yet profound communication transcended the need for words. In that moment, in the midst of the ER's chaos, it was as if he was a guardian angel sent to affirm my strength, to remind me to hold on to hope.

The head physician's words still echoed in my ears as he mentioned summoning their top spine surgeon for an emergency operation at dawn. A surge of panic washed over me once more. I glanced through the curtain, searching for the comforting presence of the old man, but he had disappeared. Isolation gripped me and fear crept in, settling heavily on my chest. The doctor entered the room while I was still under the influence of the pain medication—conscious yet drowsy. "Emi," he began, addressing me with a calm yet serious tone, "I'll be performing your operation. It's important for you to understand that there are certain risks involved, including the possibility of paralysis." That fear still lingered at the forefront of my mind. Nevertheless, he confidently conveyed his record of success with such procedures and stressed that this surgery was the critical solution needed to alleviate the unbearable pain in my back, chest, and arms. As I drifted back into a state of unconsciousness, I briefly registered his parting words that there was a possibility of losing the ability to speak, a rare but real risk hovering around three percent. At that moment, paralysis was my primary fear, overshadowing any concern for my speech. In hindsight, I wish I had been able to push myself to ask more about that three percent risk.

———

My voice was the heartbeat of the Foundation; telling my story and speaking about the work we were doing was one of my chief responsibilities. I had a slew of speaking engagements scheduled for the upcoming fall and winter. We were sold out for upcoming events. Awakening, my eyes fluttered open to the unexpected sight of my sister, who had flown in from Florida; her presence was an immediate joy. I opened my mouth to say hello, but nothing came out. My voice was gone.

For several days, I was confined to a hospital bed under strict orders of silence. The physicians surmised that my vocal cords required a brief respite for recovery. Yet, as the days stretched into weeks and eventually months, my voice failed to make its return. In its place remained a squeaky, high-pitched echo reminiscent of Minnie Mouse; it was as discomforting to wield as it was grating to hear. I was facing a dilemma with forthcoming speaking engagements for companies who had sponsored events, and uncertain how I would fulfill these commitments. Embarking on vocal therapy, I found myself growing frustrated as I echoed 'la la la' across various pitches, feeling the minutes tick by. With work already set aside for a week due to surgery and healing, these seemingly trivial exercises frayed my nerves. However, the medical team cautioned patience, emphasizing that the journey to regain my voice could span six to twelve months.

Upon my return to the Factory in our basement, the pace hadn't slowed; our living room was now transformed into my makeshift office, with a beach lounge chair as my unconventional command center. My agility was severely restricted by the neck brace encasing my head, prohibiting

any semblance of movement—a stark contrast to the dynamism of my life just a week prior, filled with event hosting and engaging with volunteers on the road. We deftly rescheduled the forthcoming events without revealing the fact that I had suffered an injury so severe it robbed me of my ability to communicate.

Following an intense battle marked by months of silence due to vocal cord damage sustained during emergency surgery, I now began to face significant challenges with breathing and swallowing. My persistent search led me to a specialist at Mass Eye and Ear, who performed a vocal cord injection. The procedure was a turning point, alleviating some of my discomfort and, crucially, restoring my ability to speak.

By now, Wendy was regularly commuting between Baltimore and Massachusetts, lending her aid over weekends and any spare vacation time. It was during one of these trips that I explained the dire need of a larger space with adequate storage and room for volunteers to assist us in prepping Happy Hope Boxes. And with that, Wendy was on it. She enlisted her friend Denise, a maestro of design, and both swooped in the following week to scout for our inaugural Happy Hope Factory. I've always had faith that when everything aligns just right, miracles tend to unfold. The journey to building out the Happy Hope Factory had been filled with serendipitous encounters and remarkable milestones, reinforcing my conviction that Conor's guidance was a fateful force behind this entire endeavor.

We stumbled upon our ideal venue within a week—an unassuming space crowded by a maze of vacant cubicles that also housed a perfectly sized warehouse, at 6 Benjamin Nye Circle in Pocasset, Massachusetts. To many, it may not have been an obvious choice, but it was evident to me; this was where our roots would grow. Denise rapidly mapped out a visionary blueprint. Her design transformed the space into a vibrant community hub complete with an inviting entry, a community center equipped with top-tier audiovisual technology, an in-house print station, a boutique gift shop, and the Connection Center for our communications team. Furthermore, it included a dedicated area for assembling Happy Hope Boxes, a comprehensive storage facility, kitchen, restrooms, with every corner diligently designed for optimal use. This would be our new home: the Happy Hope Factory.

In the ensuing months, we managed the transition, shuttling inventory from the basement to the Factory amid the hustle of fulfilling an ever-growing number of Happy Hope Box orders. It became glaringly evident that I was in over my head;

the operation was expanding, and my skillset in strategic operations was not adequate for the scale at which we were now operating. Keenly aware of this gap, I knew the solution was to find someone who could complement my strengths and take the reins on operations. There was only one candidate for this role who would be my ideal counterpart—Wendy. But the prospect of convincing her to leave a stable, hard-earned career trajectory as well as relocate her life to Massachusetts was not going to be a quick ask.

Eventually I gathered my courage and reached out to her, "Wendy, I'm in need of your guidance." I began, with her reassuring me that she had my back in this. "It's more than that. I want you onboard with us, as a permanent fixture. I'm incomplete without you, and frankly, I don't want to proceed without you." Unfortunately for me, Wendy had recently semi-retired and taken up a role with a major non-profit in Baltimore. "I've given my word for a six-month tenure here; it's only been two months. I can't simply walk away, I intended to be here for at least three years." She was saying no, but there was something in her voice that gave me a little bit of hope.

In the end, Wendy's tenure lasted precisely six months to the day. Her arrival the following day marked one of the utmost joyful days of my life, for I knew the foundation's heart was now complete with her by my side. The foundation was no longer my passion project, scraping together what I could to bring hope to as many children possible; we were a team, building on each other's strengths to nurture and grow our staff, volunteers, programs, and impact.

Chapter 9

New England had yet to warm up after a typically frosty winter, and Wendy and I were happy to leave that all behind for a few days while we traveled to Miami to host an event with NBC Telemundo. Since Wendy had come on board, our events calendar had really filled up and we were beginning to perfect our events experience. While I took on the role of presenter and storyteller, Wendy expertly managed all logistical aspects. Our skills were perfectly complementary; it was quite extraordinary to work with someone who seemed that they could nearly read my mind.

This trip would mark a small milestone for the two of us. We had built a true friendship, I trusted her guidance implicitly, and we had cohosted a number of events—but we had never traveled together. Regardless of who, traveling with another person can be a real test of one's relationship. And on this trip, we would be flying together as well as sharing a hotel room. At this time, Wendy was single, having recently ended a relationship with her girlfriend. Before we made our reservation, she made a point to ask me, "Emi, are you sure you are okay sharing a room with me?"

Of course, it was no issue to me, but I couldn't help gently tease, "just so we're clear, I'm happily married. To a man." Wendy was quick to retort, "oh please, don't flatter yourself. You're totally not my type." Thus, the matter was settled, and we booked our room, eager to break out our warm weather clothes for a few days in the sunshine.

As we stepped off the plane in Florida, eager to have a fun dinner out before putting in a long workday the next day, I stole a quick glance over at Wendy. A few days before our departure, Wendy had gone for a necessary "minor" procedure with her dermatologist. She came back from her appointment with a startling 67 stitches that made a thick line from her brow to the corner of her lip. I half-jokingly wondered how I could possibly bring her with me in such a state, and to south Florida of all places, a locale not exactly friendly to individuals previously diagnosed with skin cancer. Wendy waved off my concerns, describing how the stitches would fade by the time of our event and how she'd be sure to pack the highest spf sunscreen she could find.

As promised, the stitches had faded by the time of our flight— though I had packed extra concealer, just in case. Stepping off the plane, we beelined it for baggage claim, excited to get on with our evening. And there we stood, waiting and waiting until it was clear that all bags from our flight had been unloaded and claimed. "Are you f****** kidding me?" she exclaimed as we both realized we had no clothes for our big event tomorrow, nor toiletries, not even a toothbrush.

"We'll just have to hit up a nearby TJ Maxx or Target," I suggested optimistically. "Emi, there's no chance this girl is going to find something at this hour from Target or TJ Maxx. We need to head straight to Macy's," she shot back with urgency. Once there, Wendy headed straight for the women's section, finding racks upon racks of vibrant Miami fashion—clothing with audacious cutouts, generously embellished with sparkling rhinestones and assorted gems. As she modeled a series of increasingly loud ensembles for me, I could barely catch my breath from laughter. "Emi, I look like I'm in a much different line of work, if you catch my drift." Oh, I did.

The evening's shopping frenzy had us parting with a significant $300 each, as the ticking clock pressured our choices just before the store's imminent closure. Once laden with bags, we ventured back to our vehicle, a hint of hope in my voice as I mused over a brighter start in Miami the next day. Indeed, the following day exceeded expectations with its triumphs, leading us to our next event as we cruised along the Miami strip in our convertible Mustang, the breeze tugging at Wendy's cap. It didn't take long, however, to notice that we were now amidst a sea of revelers, having unwittingly timed our trip with the height of collegiate Spring Break.

After a lovely dinner near our hotel, and some time spent decompressing and browsing Wendy's dismal Match.com prospects back in Massachusetts, we woke up ready to greet the day and join another team in packing Happy Hope Bags for children in Miami.

Upon our arrival, however, the coordinator greeted us with news of an unforeseen change of plans. The event we were to facilitate that day was for a medical conference that had brought in world renown physicians from across the globe. Groundbreaking research and breakthroughs in treatments were to be presented throughout the day, but no one else had accounted for the parade of scantily clad coeds passing by the conference room windows wearing barely-there bikinis. As we peered into the room, a number of young ladies were congregating against the glass walls behind the podium, making for a very distracting sight. Thus, the conference was to be relocated down the street. The new space was on the 13th floor and all of the window blinds were firmly closed, creating a more focused yet totally depressing environment for the conference goers who knew the sun was brightly shining outside. Nevertheless, we did our best to transform the space into a room filled with a different sort of sunshine. After all, and as we've always believed, one can share hope from any location.

———

On the heels of our Miami adventure, we journeyed to Nebraska to the headquarters of Oriental Trading, the epicenter of creation for products manufactured specifically for Happy Hope Bags. Imagining it as anything less than Santa's workshop does not do it justice — it's a veritable fantasy of logistics with toys cascading down chutes and a labyrinth of conveyor belts, all combining to craft a whirlwind of joyful chaos. For years we had collaborated with this manufacturing plant, and finally, we had the opportunity to observe our products' journey from sketch to tangible item.

After an enlightening day in R&D, we concluded our visit just as the evening began to settle. Eager to savor the culinary delights of the locale, we ventured to a nearby mall reputed for its diverse eateries. Post feasting, with spirits high, we meandered through the mall, our curiosity leading us into various shops. It was then, after our pedometers proudly displayed 24,000 steps, that we stumbled upon an oasis for our weary feet—a massage parlor promising the sweet relief of a foot rub, its inviting glow too tempting to resist. I felt a little uneasy at the heavy curtains, single neon sign, and darkened entrance—but desperation took over and we went inside.

After our feet had been tenderly massaged for a quarter of an hour, they draped warm towels over our eyes, stirring a hint of suspicion in me about what might follow. "Wendy," I whispered, "perhaps we should leave now." But she reassured me, "Oh, relax, Emi. Nobody's going to hurt us." That's when another presence in the room made itself known. I swiftly removed the towel from my face to see a towering woman emerging from behind a curtain. "You," she pointed directly at me, "Come with me. Keep your clothes on and lie down on the table." There, in an area concealed by more curtains, lay two adjacent tables; I was beyond glad to know I wasn't going to be alone in there. All I wanted was to run back to my car, even with wet feet notwithstanding. But, of course, Wendy was correct, and the visit was far less nefarious than I had built it up in my mind. The establishment was decent, and despite the unusual sensation of receiving a massage over our clothing, it was all over with fairly quickly. Personally, I was relieved; my time at that massage parlor had run its course but even still, I'm glad I put my faith in Wendy and left my comfort zone albeit temporarily.

———

As we journeyed far and wide, orchestrating Happy Hope Factory events, we met a number of extraordinary individuals, each with their unique and inspirational stories of hope, courage, tenacity, and resilience. These individuals have shared their touching narratives with us including parents joining us to pack Hope Bags whose children had received a bag prior to their passing and even children who had been laid to rest with their bag as these simple gifts were the final reminder of a community that cared. Our hospital partners have reached out, emphasizing the significance of items we often overlook, like toothbrushes and the stories of children sharing these essentials due to limited resources. We have packed bags on Zoom events where parents in the hospital with their own children are packing Happy Hope Bags for other children in need of hope. Stories like these profoundly move us, serving as poignant reminders of our capacity to make a significant positive impact on the lives of those around us, particularly since we never know what the future holds.

The increase in cross-country travel sparked countless encounters, transforming strangers into friends in the close quarters of planes, trains, and taxis. We often felt as though we were impromptu therapists in fleeting sessions, a role that underscored a universal truth that each person carries a unique story. What stood out was the deep-seated desire for recognition, empathy, and significance that threaded through each conversation. Everyone we were meeting wanted to know that they mattered.

Nonetheless, our work has frequently been peppered with moments where strangers would unreservedly open up about deeply personal concerns, prompting me to cast a meaningful glance towards Wendy—a silent signal she had become adept at deciphering. Through countless shared experiences, we had developed an unspoken understanding, a nonverbal dialogue that was almost telepathic. With just one look, even from across the room, Wendy could nearly always predict my thoughts and anticipate the forthcoming situation. This profound level of familiarity was not just remarkable, it was vital to working in tandem towards a common goal.

Wendy's innate ability to smooth over rocky situations or turn new acquaintances into instant friends was something I deeply respected. Her heart knows no barriers towards race, gender, age, or ability; she simply sees people, embracing diversity and advocating for those less fortunate.

Her encouragement has also never been reserved just for friends; she is the first to applaud her rivals, demonstrating a sportsmanship that's rare to encounter. Surrounding myself with individuals like Wendy, who continuously challenge norms, strive for excellence, and elevate expectations, has been an immeasurable gift she's bestowed upon me. In return, I've aimed to show her how a bit of softness and compassion can brighten the world without compromising one's ambition to succeed. Our shared laughter is the sort that erupts from the very core of your being, travels through your spirit, and bursts forth in a cascade of uncontrollable joy, leaving your eyes gleaming with tears from the uproarious imagery dancing around in your thoughts. Understanding Wendy means being ready for the unexpected, like the memorable journey back home on a Friday afternoon from San Fransisco.

After a seemingly endless sequence of Hope Factory engagements across the Golden State, we were drained to our core. Barely a shred of energy remained as we staggered back into our hotel room, famished and half-joking about the prospect of gnawing on our own limbs. Succumbing to sheer necessity, we did what anyone in our worn-out shoes would do: order room service. Our anticipated feast: two juicy hamburgers, a side of fries, and the comforting fizz of a Coca-Cola. It was the epitome of comfort, despite the agonizing two-hour wait it entailed. Stuffed to the brim, we succumbed to sleep, barely managing a cursory brush of our teeth. The week's triumphs had taken their toll, culminating in a lapse that seasoned travelers dread: the Southwest Airlines seating scramble. Forgetting to check in at the 24-hour mark meant surrendering any hope of a decent boarding spot. When passengers C59 and C60 woke the next day, the error dawned upon us and Wendy's frustration flared, "Emi, how could you forget?!" But I was quick to retort, "Hey, you could've remembered, too." Our laughter diffused the tension; we knew what the future held all too well: stranded in the back, sandwiched between strangers in two decidedly snug middle seats, on opposite sides of the aisle.

Stepping onto the aircraft, Wendy made a beeline for the rear as instructed by the flight attendant. Yet as Wendy proceeded down the aisle, a curiosity caught my attention—an unoccupied middle seat in the premium front row, strangely vacant. There I stood, the final passenger to board, puzzled by the empty space. My mind raced with possible explanations: a spill, a mess, something to deter others. I paused, eyeing the seat and the woman sitting by the window, her professional attire a familiar echo of the corporate world that offered a sense of ease. "Pardon me, is this seat occupied?" I inquired. "No, it's reserved for you," came the reply, accompanied by a warm smile. Stowing my items in the overhead compartment, I settled into the seat with ease. We exchanged friendly small talk, and a sense of fortune washed over me. Meanwhile, I imagined poor Wendy had likely found herself stuck between two less-than-pleasant companions at the rear, while I reclined at the front, primed for an engaging chat with my newfound acquaintance.

As I nestled into my seat, unfurling my cherished pink blanket edged with shiny satin, the woman next to me commented on it. It's my comfort object—my little piece of home that accompanies me on all my journeys, especially flights. Amidst her chuckles and the roar of the aircraft ascending towards Boston, I found my mind wandering to her life's narrative. Wendy and I had a tradition of a curious game, where we'd each unearth an intriguing backstory from our seatmate and later exchange our findings over a meal. It often ended with the realization that those around us, much like us, yearned to simply be heard.

"Are you returning home?" I turned to my seatmate to make a little small talk. We began chatting and then the woman posed to me a very unexpected question of her own. "Is it okay if I call you Vanilla?" she asked. "Vanilla?" I echoed, puzzled. Not fully grasping her intent and cautious of causing any upset, I acquiesced. Still not quite sure what to make of my new nickname, I steered the conversation towards her weekend plans, "Do you have anything fun scheduled for the next few days?" I inquired. "Yes, I do," she responded. "I'm getting collared."

Puzzled yet again, I asked for clarification, which in hindsight was a mistake. She began sharing that although she typically served as more of a dominatrix, she was about to move into being an attendant to a dominatrix of her own. She then gestured towards the overhead compartment. Somewhat bewildered and slightly afraid of her reaction if I did not comply, I retrieved her oversized duffle bag, which clattered with all sorts of noisy, peculiar items. Upon unzipping the bag, an array of bondage attire adorned with chains and a collection of exotic devices were revealed. I began to wonder again how Wendy was faring at the back of the plane. I would never have suspected that the lady sitting next to me could fit the role of a dominatrix or anything similar. She appeared more like someone who might work as an HR Director—

middle-aged, dressed conservatively. And yet, there I was, seated beside her for an unexpectedly revealing five-hour journey, murmuring compliments on the many photos of her decked out in leather and chains that she shared.

"There's a dungeon in every neighborhood, Vanilla," she proclaimed as we disembarked. "You never really know what's happening behind closed doors." When Wendy finally emerged, last to disembark but in high spirits, I recounted the entire flight in exacting detail to her extreme delight. In stark contrast, Wendy's flight experience was the exact opposite; seated between partners commemorating their 75th wedding anniversary, her journey was replete with affection and peace. With both our tales told, we reached a consensus: investing in automatic check-in was the way forward. And as for encounters with dominatrices, that was an experience I intend to be my first and last.

———

At last, we returned to the comforting familiarity of our Happy Hope Factory in Massachusetts. Months of continuous travel had taken its toll, and the solidity of our own space was a long-awaited comfort. With a holiday weekend on the horizon, Wendy was organizing a trip to see her family in the northern reaches of New York, and our team was diligently completing the last of the orders before the forthcoming holiday respite. I had promised Wendy that I would drive her to Boston Logan Airport for her flight, so I was hurriedly finishing my tasks, powering down my computer and securing the files. "Wendy!"

I called out as lights flickered off and the hum of the printers ceased. "We've got to get on the road now, or we'll be stuck in the weekend traffic to Boston." Deep down, I knew the congested Cape roads cared little for my schedule.

I searched for Wendy, pacing down the hallway toward the restrooms. "Wendy!" I yelled once more but was greeted only by silence. It was very out of character for someone as boisterous and lively as Wendy not to respond, and a knot of concern started to form in my gut. Where on earth could she be? Rounding a corner in the hallway, I finally found her leaning hard against the wall, her head clasped in her hands. "Wendy, we need to leave, now," I urged again, but she still didn't respond.

"What's going on?" I pressed, crouching by her side, my pulse thudding in my ears. Her silence persisted. "Wendy!" I called out louder this time. When her eyes met mine, I got an immediate sense of the crisis. A shout for help brought another employee sprinting. "Get an ambulance," I barked. I turned back to Wendy and instructed her, "Point to your nose for me." Her fingertip's misguided journey towards her ear was all I needed to see.

Within a few minutes, the paramedics swarmed in with urgent precision, swiftly assessing her condition and securing her onto the stretcher. As the ambulance doors closed, I assured them I would trail them to the hospital, my gut twisting with dread. She was more than a business partner; she was the companion with whom I had tirelessly built our dream, our factory. The sheer possibility of forging ahead without her was terrifying; I grappled with my emotions, barely reining in tears amidst the tumultuous thoughts of uncertainty. Shadowing the urgent wail of the sirens, a surge of panic washed over me, leaving me to ponder if I, too, might collapse upon arrival at the emergency room.

Several hours of anxious pacing in the emergency room waiting area eased as I was beckoned into the room where Wendy, amidst a nest of sterile hospital linen, appeared drained but

present. "Emi, what's going on? Why this room, and oh, hey, could you find those hospital socks? It's like the Arctic in here for my toes!" The sound of her voice, tinged with her characteristic humor, offered a speck of normality 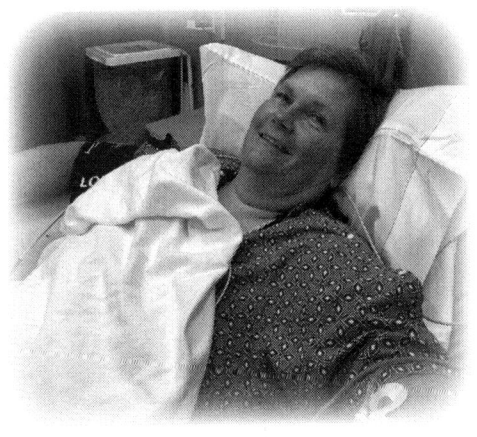 amidst the chaos. I couldn't help but laugh as I slipped the socks onto her feet. "Wendy, can you point to your nose for me?" I inquired, repeating the simple test. "You think I don't know where my own nose is?" she retorted, apparently unaware that just a few hours earlier she'd been uncertain of the exact location.

The doctors diagnosed her with a TIA—a transient ischemic attack, often referred to as a mini-stroke; essentially, a brief interruption of blood flow to the brain. Wendy's stay in the hospital was anything but tranquil; she became notorious for disconnecting her monitors to sneak into a quiet bathroom break and was constantly questing for culinary alternatives to the dreary hospital fare. Eventually, after causing a minor commotion for a few days, she was discharged, continuing her recovery under the familiar roof of our home. "Emi, there's one other thing I need. We should really consider giving a generous donation to the ambulance service." She couldn't stop giggling. "I'm positive they needed to hose down that ambulance after they dropped me off. They handed me a tiny bag as if that could possibly contain that calamity; they really should have heeded my warning. So, yes, let's send them a little something."

Chapter 10

Wendy's resilience has always mirrored that of a proverbial cat with its fabled nine lives. Over the last four decades, she's navigated a labyrinth of health challenges—a brain tumor extraction, repeated skin cancer treatments, and a separate cancer diagnosis three times. Despite these trials, Wendy's tenacity has never wavered. She confronts each new obstacle with a fierce determination, refusing to allow her vibrancy to be overshadowed by self-pity. Witnessing Wendy maintain her upbeat spirit in the face of difficulties has often reminded me of observing the struggles and triumphs of children in hospitals; it's clear that adversity presents us with a critical choice. We can succumb to bitterness over our circumstances, or we can strive to rise above them. But how, really, does one cultivate a positive attitude during life's most challenging moments?

That pivotal February day, forever ago, altered the landscape of my existence. The ensuing years were full of some of the hardest days, with no choice but to keep going on to the next. It's an existence familiar to so many of the families we serve. The toughest phases of my journey taught me to rethink difficulties as opportunities; opportunities that many of my educators doubted due to my severe reading disabilities.

Through observing Conor's daily struggles, I've come to realize that grit and relentless perseverance are just as important as natural talent. No matter how long or arduous the journey from point A to point B is, no matter how steep and deep the path meanders, the willingness to overcome adversity is one of the most potent tools one can possess. Recognize that you are significant, your existence is meaningful, and your life is intricately crafted for a purpose far greater than what's on the surface. You have the power to redefine your life and what you value at any point. The opportunity for change exists up until the very end, so as long as life endures, it's within your capacity to focus on the pursuit of genuine joy—an endeavor that is deeply personal and entirely in your hands. Take this moment now to embrace the search for happiness, for your joy, for your purpose.

————

It has been nearly thirteen years now, and I still think of Wendy every time I pass a tomato display at a grocery store. There was a time when I perceived her as the lion and myself merely as the mouse. Yet, as our journey unfolded, I realized the profound truths we shared. We have become each other's greatest teachers, embraced our differences and celebrated our strengths. Wendy embodies the beautiful sentiment that "all boats rise together." Through her wisdom, I have learned that we can elevate one another, nurturing a bond that thrives on support and encouragement rather than competition and discord. Each lesson we've imparted has woven a tapestry of resilience and empowerment, reminding me that true strength lies in unity. I've since come to realize that this hasn't been a one-sided journey. Wendy has been my Yoda, showing me business lessons that no MBA program could ever impart. But it's a two-way street. Her heart has grown exponentially as she prioritizes purpose over profit, using her talents to make a real difference. Seeing

her conjure her daily magic in the factory, I know she is exactly where she needs to be. And isn't that the greatest feeling?

As I look back on my path—maneuvering the hurdles of academia, observing the profound impact my father had on his patients, crossing paths with Wendy, learning about beauty and color in my grandmother's garden —I feel deep appreciation for the guidance these moments and individuals provided to me. These life experiences, from the highest highs to the most devastating lows, are equally important steps along our paths, and it's how we decide to utilize them that shapes our journey. Harnessing the power of hope is essential in this process, as it allows us to tap into the joy that resides deep within.

I wish for you to always remember that nothing is impossible. In the moments when uncertainty looms like a dark cloud overhead, when life feels heavy with challenges that seem insurmountable, hold onto this truth: the very word "impossible" can be transformed. It whispers to us, saying, "I'm possible." This powerful reminder can light a spark of hope, urging you to embrace the journey ahead with courage and determination. Remember, every doubt you face is an opportunity to rise, to redefine your limits, and to discover just how extraordinary you can truly be. Understand your value, exude your innate power, live your life filled with intention, and become a beacon of inspiration for those navigating their own paths. Every day presents us with chances to positively impact others' lives. There's no necessity to delay, as the present moment is the most opportune time to uplift, empower, and be the catalyst for the positive transformations our world seeks. All the gifts you possess are powerful enough to make a significant impact, so step out and let your light shine. You matter, and without a doubt, **you are extraordinary**!

In closing...

Growing up in a small town in upstate NY, I learned the value of hard work early in life. My father was a perfectionist; whether hosing down the restaurant parking lot or making a Manhattan, it all needed to be just so.

I learned to love hard work and assumed happiness and success would resonate from it. As a milestone birthday approached one year, I had been wondering what might be next for me. It turned out not to be a gift or a thing that would mark my next era; it was a chance meeting with a woman and her son. I had worked my entire life for profit and now had the chance to work for purpose. As I learned from Conor and Emi, my life was blessed beyond measure. What is the secret to a happy and successful life? Contrary to what you might think, it's not career achievement, money, exercise, or a healthy diet. It's positive, meaningful relationships. What started over tomatoes has blossomed into a mutual friendship and a successful nonprofit sharing the power of doing good. We hope you have enjoyed this chapter in our lives, and we look forward to sharing what's next!

The story continues with laughter, hope, and light.

– Wendy Webster

> "The only mistake in life is the
> lesson not learned."
>
> ~ Albert Einstein

NOTES

_____

_____

_____

_____

_____

_____

_____

_____

_____

_____

_____

_____

The chapters in this book mirror the chapters
of our lives, each page filled with uncertainty yet
brimming with possibility. We all begin on page one as
we embark on a remarkable journey, aware that every
new section is a vital thread woven into the fabric of
our existence. Discovering our purpose, igniting our
passion, and heeding the whispers of our hearts guide
us toward the extraordinary narrative we long to create.
We challenge you to embrace your heart's desires, to
venture into the unknown without fear, and to always
extend kindness to others. Together, let us craft the story
of our lives with courage and compassion, making every
chapter a reflection of our deepest truths.
Remember your why!